A SLIP FROM GRACE

More tales from Little Ireland

SEAN CLOSE

Close Publishing

DEDICATION

I would like to dedicate this book to my wife, Joan. She didn't know me at the time, but fell in love with the person I became. I love you, Joan.

Published by Close Publishing
1 Wynfield Parks Road, Arlecdon, Frizington, Cumbria CA26 3XF
closepublishing@aol.com

Typeset and designed by Questa Publishing
PO Box 520, Bamber Bridge, Preston, Lancashire PR5 8LF

Printed by Printexpress (Cumbria) Limited, Whitehaven, Cumbria
Front cover designed by Printexpress (Cumbria) Limited

CONTENTS

ACKNOWLEDGEMENTS

Since the publication in 2001 of my first book *Little Ireland: Memories of a Cleator Childhood,* I have been inundated with messages of congratulations from all corners of the globe. Many have been from ex-patriots of Cleator Moor who were sent copies of the book by their family or friends. It has made me realise how many people have left our area to find fame and fortune elsewhere. It's a bit like the exodus of Ireland, but on a smaller scale.

I have been contacted by numerous relatives of my own, both in England and abroad. Prior to the publication of the book I was unaware of the existence of many of these relatives. They have all written with fond memories of Cleator Moor, speaking of it as a very special place. And yet they all had left it behind...why is this?

I was pleased that I was able to give them a reminder and a flavour of 'Little Ireland', as I remember it, and would like to thank all these people, and hope this second book will also find its way to them and provoke similar feelings.

I would like to thank my family and friends for their constant help and encouragement.

Finally, I would like to thank the characters who appear in the book and their inspirational input. Some names have been changed in order not to offend. If any offence is caused in spite of these measures, I apologise in advance.

Sean Close

September 2002

FOREWORD

Not long after arriving in the Parish of St. Mary's, Cleator I had taken a day off to explore the Lakes. Driving home to the Parish I got caught in a fierce blizzard and was forced to seek refuge in Arlecdon. The house I called at was owned by a parishioner, Sean Close, the author of this book. I remember his wife Joan opening the door and, recognising me as the new priest, instantly assuming that I was bearing bad tidings. Such is the effect of priestly visits! When I explained my predicament she welcomed me in and we sat waiting for her husband to return home. During the next hour another snowbound 'refugee' arrived to be joined shortly afterwards by Sean himself. Food was prepared, beds were made up and we settled in, like siege victims, to wait the abatement of the storm.

During the course of the evening and fuelled by warming libations, our host began to regale us with stories of his past. As the new priest in the area he thought it would be helpful if I had some background information on the traditions and customs of the area to which I had been assigned. And what stories they were! Suddenly a rich world of colourful characters was opened up to me. We listened raptly until the small hours. Sadly my host's generosity with the "warming libations" left me befuddled and confused the next morning and much of what he had told me the night before was reduced to a kaleidoscope of disjointed memories. It was with great joy, therefore, that I encountered his first book and was able, at a more leisurely pace and with clear head, to reacquaint myself with his reminiscences or rural parish life. And now .... more of the same.

Together, this book forms a valuable insight into a world that once was; a world of innocent pleasures and community spirit; of corner stores and larger than life local characters; when doors were left unlocked and children and the elderly could walk the streets unmolested. What little remains of those times lives on in the hearts and memories of many who will find this book an invaluable and humorous addition to their own recollections. For those who did not live through those times it is a painful reminder that whilst progress has brought much that is good, it has served to erode much that was of value, not least a sense of community and collective responsibility.

As I leave the Parish of St. Mary's, Cleator after seven years of ministry, I am honoured to have been asked to write this foreword, for I have my own treasured memories of the people and the area in which I have been privileged to serve.

Rev. William Glasswell

Assistant Priest

4th November 2002

PREFACE

This book rides on the back of my first book *Little Ireland: Memories of a Cleator Childhood*. It chronicles my early teenage years and describes a wealth of new characters and adventures resulting from my family's move from the sleepy village of Cleator, to Cleator Moor. Say 'Goodbye' to the oppressive 1950s and 'Hello' to the swinging Sixties and the Permissive Society (raging hormones and all!). I was privileged to enjoy a rich Irish heritage and now had to adapt it to my new surroundings.

The 1960s were no longer thought of as the Post War years. We had done all that. The war was hardly ever mentioned – my generation had deposited it in the dustbin of history. Our most recent history was space travel and pogo sticks. We were experiencing supersonic air travel, the Beatles and polystyrene (well, not me personally!).

These pages encapsulate my transition from an innocent boy of ten to a less-than-innocent bof of fifteen. We are all biologically programmed to reproduce ourselves, and most of us manage to do it. The fascinating thing to me is how we achieve this, and the process it takes. Our social structure tries its best to stop us doing this for as long as possible. Between the ages of ten and fifteen we learn about the process, and then by a greater or lesser degree we eventually do it.

So, please, lighten up and come back in time with me once again, to a time when little boys started to wear long pants and little girls always said 'No.'

CHAPTER 1
SEAVIEW PLACE
WITHOUT A SEA VIEW

We had been living at 12 Croasdale Place for over a year now and Dad wanted more garden space. He had put a hut in the back garden and that had taken at least a third of the garden space and completely dominated the view from the kitchen window. So, when word got out that the Stokeses from number 7, Seaview Place were moving to a bungalow they had built at Clintz, Dad decided to put in for a swap. Mam wasn't so keen because she'd just got the house completely redecorated and carpeted and didn't really fancy the upheaval so soon after moving in.

She could see the sense in moving over the backs to Seaview Place, because number 7 was a corner house, unlike 12 Croasdale, which was in the middle of a row. All the corner houses had much bigger gardens and we would be back to back with Auntie Lily, so that would be handy. We could cut a gate into the fence between us and have access across the gardens. So it was settled: an application to the Council was sent in and accepted really without any problems at all.

As soon as the Stokeses moved out, we moved in. We literally passed everything into the new house from the old one over the fence from back garden to back garden. No removal van was necessary. All the neighbours helped and we were settled in within the day. Mam was dreading having to start again with the decorating, but at least the carpets fitted without much alteration. Luckily the Seaview house was a fraction smaller than the Croasdale house, so that was in our favour as far as the carpets were concerned. The Seaview house was generally better situated, because the front was high up and overlooked the car park through the gap in the houses in front of it, so it didn't seem so cramped, but where the hell the sea view was to be had was a complete mystery.

The local council was responsible for naming the avenues and streets of the new estates, which were springing up everywhere at Cleator Moor with alarming regularity. Our estate had been completed within three years, from cutting the first sod to handing the keys to the last tenant on Priory Drive. Some seventy-odd houses, a sort of village within a village. Somehow we had our own identity.

The Sub-Committee responsible for naming the streets of our estate must have started off with some sort of local theme in mind. The first cul-de-sac to be built was named Kinniside Place, after the local fell by the same name. Then came Croasdale Place, again named after a local beauty spot near Ennerdale. The theme continued with Priory Drive; not so obvious, but relating to the Priory nearby at Cleator. But then they absolutely lost the plot with Seaview Place.

Honest to God, there is no sign of the sea, not a single glimpse, not even a distant view of the sea which is five miles away as the crow flies. So, what could be the possible connection? Except maybe a bit of poetic licence was used to give the estate a more cosmopolitan feel, or as I suspect, they got the names mixed up with the next new estate being built nearby. This estate would have a row of houses called Melbreak Avenue, Melbreak being another local hillock of outstanding beauty which would have fitted in with the local theme, and it is possible to get a glimpse of the sea from Melbreak Avenue on the rare occasion of the sky being clear enough to detect the strip of blue between Egremont and Moor Row.

The next new estate would have names like Greenthwaite, Thornfield and Longbarrow. The locally named Melbreak Avenue was out of tune with the theme of the more obscure Thwaites and Fields theme. I'm sure that's what happened, but of course, no-one will ever admit it now, so we should really be living at number 7, Melbreak Avenue, not Seaview Place.

I rest my case.

Actually, I should feel rather lucky because the council houses built just prior to our estate had been given more radical labourite street names such as Kier Hardie Avenue and Robert Owen Avenue. If our estate had been built ten years or so later, we could be living at Nelson Mandela Crescent or Che Guevara Crossings to keep pace with political correctness. Anyhow, I'll look with interest when any more new estates are planned.

Our new home was really very conveniently situated. Our new School, St Cuthbert's RC Secondary Modern, was almost within spitting distance and the Catholic Church, St Mary's, was only five minutes walk away; even nearer than when we lived at Cleator village. All the shops were handy for Mam and we were on a very regular bus route for Whitehaven. So all in all, Cleator Moor was proving to be a very good move.

Moving house at eleven years of age is ideal for many reasons. For a start you have to change schools anyhow, so it doesn't interrupt your education and it is a great age to make new mates. The whole social interaction of getting to know neighbours and finding out who is who, who comes from where, who to avoid and who was a 'must' to get to know was a fascinating experience to me. One into which I threw myself with fevered enthusiasm.

Having been part of a very tightly knit community at Cleator, I was keen to explore and expand my knowledge of the rich seam of new neighbours I found myself amongst. Only a handful of relatives from Cleator had moved to the new estate, so I had limitless new acquaintances to make. The brain of an eleven-year-old is like a sponge absorbing information. In less than three months, I had the pedigrees and backgrounds of just about everybody, young and old. Family backgrounds gleaned from conversations overheard between Mam and Auntie Lily. Visits from Nana Heron and Papa, recognising neighbours from across the street, dropping little bits of information you don't realise you're picking up, but you do.

I was on a roll and there was no stopping me.

Mam more or less gave us free rein at choosing our friends. She approved of Malcolm and Alan Tate who lived at 13 Croasdale Place, our first neighbours. Not Catholics mind you, but you can't have everything. They were from a decent family, so that was the main thing, believe it or not. In fact, Mrs Tate was very much Church of England, even to the extent of going to Church at Wath Brow Mission every Sunday, which wasn't the practice of most Protestants. So a sneaking regard for her display of Christianity was held by Mam, although she never actually admitted it.

Malcolm and Alan were a bit too over-mothered I thought. I mean if they had a cold they had to stay in bed, and they had very strict bed times and going home times. We had rules in our house, but they were a lot more flexible than theirs. Our rules were more like Mam saying when we went out to play after school 'Mind you're back before it gets too dark' and our bedtime was any time between eight o'clock and half past nine depending on how tired we were, whilst theirs was strictly half past eight on the dot. When we had a cold we coughed and sneezed and snottered all over the place until it finally dried up. We never spent a single minute of it in our beds. So there you are, as my Mam would say. They were fussy Protestants, end of story.

Our Stephen, Malcolm and me had spent night after night after school practising our manoeuvres on the roller skates. The new estate offered limitless slalom runs down the newly tarmaced roads and paths around the cul-de-sacs. The surfaces were as smooth as a billiard table and our best run was from the top of Kinniside Place, down the full length of Priory Drive, turning left into Seaview Place and the final descent with your knees bent and your arms wrapped round them to hold your crouched position, finally to stop sharp on the rough gravel at the car park on Sea View Place. We could turn circles at high speed, jump over hurdles in the road and land at high speed on the other side. There weren't many cars, so we could leave the hurdles there while we traversed back up the hill to start again.

CHAPTER 2
TANTA JACQUES

After a bellyfull of the roller skates and knees full of scabs, we needed to try some gentler pastime for a while. So it was decided we'd try our hand at a bit of shoplifting. Now, when I say shoplifting, this experience was going to be a one-off, just for a laugh. I mean, we never thought of it as being like proper stealing. We'd heard all about it and it sounded like something we should at least try out.

The plan was this: Tanta Jacques had a wee sweet shop at the end of Ennerdale Road near Wath Brow corner and he'd just opened a café. Well, I say a café, but really it was just a corner of the shop with one table and two chairs. It had a curtain in front of it to screen the would-be diners from the main shop. The main shop (it sounds rather grand) was in fact only one room and had originally been the front parlour of the house, so you can imagine the size of it. You couldn't swing a cat in it. I'm not kidding, the counter took up two thirds of the floor space.

You walked in through the shop door and you had six feet by three feet of floor space. Then, to your right was a wooden partition only three feet long and behind this was the 'café'. It was no bigger than our outside lavatory at Cleator and it smelt a bit like it as well. Now, who the hell was going to sit there and have a cup of tea and one of Tanta's homemade rock buns, I ask you?

He was a good laugh mind, was Tanta. I mean you could buy a cigarette and a match for 3d and there was no age restriction. We could hardly see over the counter and he'd sell us them. Our Stephen went in one day with some of his birthday money and asked Tanta for Ten Woodbines and Tanta ratched about for ages behind the counter. He finally blurted out 'Sorry Lad, I've only got nine left.' So Stephen, feeling sorry for him said, 'Oh well I'll just have five Tanta, I don't want to leave you with none.' To which Tanta replied 'That's good of you lad, I don't want to disappoint me regulars 'til I get me new stock in next week.' I don't know whether he was being serious or not; you never quite knew with Tanta.

Mary McCreadie

Cleator Moor being full of nutters, somebody was bound to patronise Tanta's café if only for a good laugh. We couldn't wait to see who would be the first to give it a go. You could have taken bets on it, as it happens. Tanta's first customer was Mary McCreadie and his second customer was the equally well-known Rooty Byres.

Poor Mary, she had at one time been a manic depressive; mind you long before we knew her. She was a laugh-a-minute to us, but at one time she wouldn't go out of the house and she couldn't talk to anybody, she was so nervous. So extreme was her depression, they decided to give her electric shock treatment and by God had it worked. She'd talk the robin off a starch box. You couldn't shut her up. People would walk half-a-mile out of their way to avoid her because she pilloried everybody and his dog. She was always ripping the bag out of the Council for something or other. She became very confrontational; in fact she'd fight with a feather for no good reason. People used to say they'd given her 15 amps instead of 5 amps by mistake, so she'd gone from one extreme to the other. I hope Tanta's rock buns are up to scratch or she'll report him to the Health Inspector at the very least.

Mary takes up her position behind the curtain and Tanta shouts, 'Are you ready to order lass?' giving us the wink at the same time.

Mary shouts back 'I'm not ready to talk to a voice without a face,' and holds her ground. So Tanta makes his way round the counter and pulls the curtain to one side. 'Now lass, what would you like? I've got a couple of pies, three or four nice drop scones, or I could make you a corned beef sandwich with crisps.'

'I'll just have a cup of coffee, please,' says Mary in quite a posh voice.

'Oh sorry, lass,' says Tanta. 'No coffee, just tea, we haven't got the coffee sorted yet, lass.'

'Excuse me,' says Mary. 'Not so much of the 'lass' if you don't mind. I'll settle for a cup of tea and a drop scone Mr Jacques, and I would like to wish you well in your new venture.'

'Well, thank you very much Missus,' says Tanta. 'Only too glad to be of service.'

While all of this was going on our plan to do some shoplifting was being acted out, although not too successfully, it has to be said. Stephen was supposed to keep Tanta talking while I ratched about with my hand behind my back on the shelf behind me. As Tanta was otherwise distracted by his very first café customer, Stephen's role in all of this was not required. This had not been part of the master plan and I couldn't be sure I was not being observed by either Tanta or Mary.

After pulling the first thing my hand landed on behind me, I rushed forward in a state of panic and presented the small package to Tanta for payment. Tanta said, 'Are you doing a wee bit of decorating lad?' Looking up to the counter and my surprise purchase, I saw a packet of Polycell wallpaper paste. I thought I had a packet of sherbet. I was speechless and Tanta said, 'Well, lad, it's what's left over from decorating the café, but I'll let you have it cheap. You see I'm only allowed to sell consumables, so keep it to yourself. Do you need a Woodbine or a No. 6 while you're here?'

I agreed to a No 6 and a match for shame's sake and wondered what we could do with the wallpaper paste. Stephen and I decided that shoplifting was not all it was cracked up to be. The rush of adrenalin that Michael Murphy spoke of felt more like a panic attack. Exhilaration didn't even come into it. I just felt sick, how could we rob poor old Tanta bare-faced in front of him while he was amusing us by taking the piss out of Mary McCreadie? No, we tried it and didn't like it. So we won't be doing it again.

The wallpaper paste wasn't wasted because we decided to paper the inside of our gang hut back to front with some old wallpaper that Mam had left over from the bedrooms. At least it wasn't a complete waste of money.

We hung about inside Tanta's for a while longer because he was about to get his second customer, Rooty Byres. Rooty was a big lump of a bloke about fortyish, who knows? He spoke like a woman. 'How you doing Mary, lass,' says Rooty, while he viewed the new emporium.

'I'm fine,' says Mary. 'Thank you very much.' This man with the woman's voice sent out too many wrong signals and I found him repugnant and a bit frightening. Although he was very friendly to me and Stephen saying 'Have you lads tried Tanta's tarts yet?' and laughing like a drain I thought he was going to spit his false teeth out. We recognised the double meaning and blushed obligingly, while Mary gave out a stifled girlish giggle.

Rooty made funeral wreaths and wedding bouquets for a living and he knitted all his own sweaters by his own admission. He had all the mannerisms of a pantomime dame and if I'm not mistaken, wearing the merest hint of rouge on his cheeks. As Mam would say, 'It takes all sorts to make a world' and 'There, but for the grace of God, go I.'

These two people made a bizarre couple, to say the least. Observing them was like glancing into a world of misfits and freaks to my young unsophisticated mind. Tanta was hell bent on having a field day of piss-taking yet again with his new punter. This time I hadn't the stomach for it. Enough is enough; it's too easy to take a rise out of unfortunates like these and I wanted no more part in it. My better judgement took us out of the shop-cum-café and onto our next adventure.

CHAPTER 3
WAS IT SUICIDE,
OR JUST A TRAGIC ACCIDENT?

Not so much an adventure as a terrible ordeal. Our Barry had gone to the 'Christian Brothers' in Bournemouth to train as a Missionary, probably to teach poor wee black babies in Africa. He was only twelve when he first went away and I thought Mam was going to go in a low way. Brother Dennis Roberts had recruited Barry from St Mary's Juniors on one of his regular recruitment drives to the local Catholic schools.

Barry had made overtures in this direction from an early age and he was bright; potentially good material for the priesthood. After a couple of years of observation by Brother Dennis, and with Barry's full approval, he left us, and our family felt as if it had been invaded and violated. There were many tears and much wondering how he was and what he was doing. Was he happy? Did he have any friends? Was he being properly cared for? Did he miss us like we missed him?

Mam tried to console us by saying it was God's will and a great honour for the family, but a light had gone out in her life. Only prayers, hard work, strength of character and the fullness of time would switch it back on again. The passing weeks and months helped us get used to our loss and the regular letters from Barry and Brother Dennis reassured us. Barry came home at the end of the three main school terms and his visits were a mixture of joy and sorrow because we knew he would be leaving us again and we'd have to make the adjustment all over again.

Cuthy O'Leary

Barry had made loads of friends and seemed very happy and outgoing. One of his friends was a Cleator Moor lad who was training for the Priesthood, but with a different order. They spent much of their time at home together. His name was Cuthy O'Leary. He was a little bit older than Barry and he became a regular visitor to our home. Cuthy was a well-built, happy, smiling lad and was always full of crack, but he became ill.

I'm not sure what his illness was, but he ended his life tragically by throwing himself out of his bedroom window at his family home on Cragg Road. We were all devastated by Cuthy's death and Barry asked Stephen and me to go with him to see Cuthy's body and to pay our respects to his family.

Mrs O'Leary greeted us at the front door and although a bit weepy she seemed to be coping with the ordeal. I was secretly terrified at having to see the dead body of our young friend and after a while we were shown to the room where he was laid out. We all stood round his coffin and said a prayer – the Our Father. Somehow we all overcame our emotions and managed to control ourselves, but deep down we were well out of control.

I gazed at his face in what seemed like a tiny coffin for such a big lad. He seemed to have shrunk in size in death. I saw the evidence of his fall on his forehead. I wanted to know why he had fallen from the window. Did he do it on purpose, or did he lose his balance? No-one seemed to mention the mechanics of his death. He was just dead and what a waste it seemed to be.

After our ordeal, we were ushered back into the living room and given a cup of tea by some neighbour or other. By this time my self-control was beginning to dissolve and I was on the point of tears, but managed to keep them back. The ritual of playing the part of a bereaved and yet functional family was being played out in front of me. I was trying to imagine how our family would be reacting if it were us and I couldn't understand how they seemed so calm. I was too young to understand any of it.

A lot of chattering and even a bit of laughter drifted through the conversation going on around me and I was stunned. I wanted to go home, but it seemed inappropriate to leave after such a short visit. People were gathering for what seemed like an organised get-together. A sort of wake. It was obvious we were expected to stay, so all three of us took a seat and listened to the many kind stories about Cuthy's life. They were celebrating his life in a strange sort of way not bemoaning his death. They were also making room for all sorts of emotions to surface for everybody's benefit.

Mrs Minogue

At one point the crack became very light-hearted, even. Mrs

Minogue was Mrs O'Leary's sister, and in attendance; she was relating a story from her childhood. Mrs Minogue was an amazing talker. She hardly ever seemed to stop for breath and she talked so fast it was hard to keep up with her.

She started by shouting into the kitchen to Mrs O'Leary. 'Do you remember the dead monkey we found at the circus, Doll?'

And Doll replied, 'Oh my God aye. Our poor mammy, Lord rest her, nearly killed us.'

Swiftly interrupted by the indomitable Mrs Minogue, 'Well, we'd gone round the back of the circus wagons for a pee and there it was; a wee dead monkey in a bright red bolero and a pillbox hat. We thought it was gorgeous, not a mark on it, just as if it was asleep.'

The whole company changed mood; we all started to laugh.

'Well,' she went on. 'Our Annie said, "Why don't we take it home with us and keep it? Nobody will want it now it's dead", you know what kids is like?'

This dialogue was going on at a great rate of knots. Her skill with the spoken word was phenomenal. You couldn't have thought about Cuthy or anything else for that matter while she was rabbiting on. She went on at length describing the scene of getting a dead monkey up the stairs without mammy seeing them and how daddy would have taken the strap to them had he caught them for bringing the bloody dead monkey into the house. As if they had room for any more monkeys, the house being full as a fitch as it was with live monkeys.

Amid a fit of laughter from the company of mourners, Mrs Minogue continued her dialogue at break-neck speed. Now she'd got her audience, there was no stopping her. 'Well, we propped it up in the middle of the bed in the back room with loads of pillows and it looked lovely. It's big brown eyes staring straight in front of it. We told mammy we were going to bed early so that we wouldn't be late getting up for Mass the following morning and she wanted to know what we were up to. We convinced her we were just tired and our Annie had been sick at the circus. So she swallowed the early night crack and let us go to bed.'

'Well, we cuddled up to it in turn the three of us and pulled its wee jacket straight, adjusted its hat and stretched its arms and legs into all sorts of positions into the early hours. Mammy shouted in to us twice to get to sleep. The next morning we were all crawling with monkey fleas. Honest to God we were bitten to bits.'

The mourners erupted once again. They had all had a couple of tots by now and were loosening up a bit. It was one of those occasions where your bladder is near your eye and you can cry from laughing too much or from sadness. Mrs Minogue was saving the day and keeping our misplaced manly pride intact.

She went on, 'The next morning, the poor wee bugger was as stiff as a board sitting bolt upright with one eye open and one shut. Jesus, it looked as if it was winking at us.' The laughing was getting out of control and Mary Eldon said, 'Maisy, for God's sake have some respect for the dead.' To which Mrs Minogue valiantly backed down and continued her monologue in a quieter voice. The fleas died on them during the course of the day. 'Monkey fleas can't live on humans,' she said.

They slept with the dead monkey for nearly a week before mammy discovered its half-decomposed and stinking carcass when she went into the lasses' bedroom to change the beds. She continued, 'Poor mammy, Lord rest her, had noticed a bad smell when she opened the bedroom door, and when she pulled the blankets back off the double bed, she got the full force of the smell and nearly passed out.'

Mrs Minogue continued, accompanied by stifled laughter from the mesmerised audience. Somebody asked her, 'What did she say to you when you came home from school?'

And she replied, 'Well she didn't wait 'till we came home, she came up to the school for us. Mrs McNamee said I had to leave the classroom, my mother wanted a word with me. Jesus, she knocked seven bells out of me all the way home. I had to put it in a sack and leave it in the back yard, then strip the bed. Mammy, Lord rest her, said Daddy would have to bury it when he came home from work and he'd get his belt off to us as soon as it was done. Poor Daddy, Lord rest him, saw the funny side and pacified Mammy, Lord rest her, but threatened us never to bring a dead animal into the house again; even if it was a monkey with a red bolero and a pillbox hat.

The Old Kevin Barry

'Aye, them were the days,' said Mrs Minogue. 'Well, they were and they weren't. We had nowt, but neither did anybody else. Do you remember Daddy, Doll, when he got fined ten shillings for singing 'Kevin Barry' on the Market Square?'

'Aye, God help him,' says Doll. 'Everybody on Fletcher Street clubbed together to pay his fine. He couldn't have found ten pence, never mind ten shillings, Lord rest him. That was the Law on Cleator Moor Market Square; no Irish rebel songs except in the pubs,' said Doll.

'Dear God, where's the harm in singing 'Kevin Barry'?' said Mrs Minogue. Mary Eldon said, 'Go on, Maisy, give us a verse of the old 'Kevin Barry', lass.' So, without a moment's hesitation, her face softened and her eyes went all dewy and this lovely wee sweet voice sang out the words :

Kevin Barry do not leave me,
Cried his broken-hearted mother as she bade her son goodbye
Just a lad of eighteen summers, yet no-one can deny
As he walked to death that morning with his head held nobly high
Another martyr for old Ireland, another murder for the Crown.

She started to sob gently. 'Poor Daddy, Lord rest him, loved the old songs and that was his favourite.'

Red Petticoats for Labour

Mind you, even a sob couldn't stop her now. She went on, 'You know, they used to hang red petticoats on clothes lines across the street on voting days. You'd have been hanged if you didn't cast your vote. You see, the Catholics, the men that is, had just got the vote and they were using it with a vengeance to get the Labour in. You know they used dead men's names and false names to vote, to be sure to get the labour in. Daddy, Lord rest him, used to say Jimmy Ward had four separate votes to his certain knowledge, but nobody ever suspected because they didn't know how many Irish men lived on the Moor because they were always coming and going.

The Protestants hated us. You couldn't get a job in the Co-op or Frank Foul's if you were a Catholic. You'd go for the interview and they'd ask you which school you went to and as soon as you said Saint Patrick's they'd say 'Well, we've nothing at present but we'll let you know.' They never did. No Catholic was ever taken on. That's why we all went away into service,' said Mrs Minogue.

The Miserable Jewess

Mrs Minogue was undaunted and steeped in a cloud of nostalgia. She went on, 'My twin sister, Maggie, and me went to Canada in 1929 and got jobs looking after four wee babbies for a Jewish family in Toronto. They paid you a pittance and we were half-starved. We got half a day off a week and we were expected to do our own washing in that time. I nearly died of consumption with the hunger and the cold, so after a year we had to come back home. The old Jew promised to give us more money and better conditions to stay because the wee kids loved us, but I was too badly to look after them.

'When I got back home the doctor said I had TB, so I spent the next six months in bed. He said that the sea journey from Canada with all the fresh air on deck was as good as six months in a sanatorium, so I suppose some good came of it.' She chuckled, 'There was more meat on a butcher's apron than on me; I had to wear an overcoat to get a shadow. I was treated and looked after at home by Mammy, Lord rest her, and given cod liver oil and malt, plenty of fresh air in the room and bed rest. I never saw a doctor after that first visit when he told me I had TB, because we couldn't afford to pay for one, but I got better, thanks be to God. Many a poor soul saw their end with TB in those days; it was a scourge. It wiped out whole families. Anyway, thank God they've got it beat now.'

She looked over at us and said, 'Your poor Auntie Maggie died of the TB, lads, and I know how she got it! I was there when Edith and Blanch Pitchford knocked her down the Town Hall steps. She knocked her hip on the wall at the bottom of the steps and the TB got into the hip bone. She died a young woman of twenty-three, Lord rest her. Your poor grandmother took Maggie to Lourdes for the cure, but it wasn't to be. In fact the journey nearly killed her, she never left her bed after she got back home. You see the Protestants used to hate us. They used to wait for us coming out of the school and batter us. We couldn't understand why they hated us so much, but they did.'

The Silent Pictures at The Hip with Nelly Ward

'Mind you, it wasn't all bad,' said Mrs Minogue, who by this time had noticed her audience had gone into a bit of a decline. 'We had the silent pictures at the Hip. Poor Nelly Ward could only read three letter words and when she sat next to me I had to read the subtitles out loud to her. By the time the picture had ended I would be nearly bloody hoarse.' to light-hearted laughter.

'Aye, and there were the waggonett trips from Fletcher Street to St Bees. We'd take a basket of fruit and pies. The kids would sit on the floor of the waggonett and the men used to get off and walk up the hills to save the horses. That was usually August Monday or May Day. Aye, and we used to swim in Hen Beck in the hot weather didn't we. Doll?' said Mrs Minogue.

'Summers were hotter in them days. Mind, when I say swim in Hen Beck, I mean the lads swam, the lasses keeped their frocks on and had to be contented with a paddle. The lads swam further up past Hen Beck Bridge in their pelts, and when they got out of the beck they'd run round the Low field 'till they were dry. We never had any towels, no such luxuries. We just used to look away while they tore around the field in the altogether.'

By now, Mrs O'Leary was a bit more settled and was seated in the middle of a crowd of neighbours. She said, in a very low soft voice, 'I remember Daddy getting his first pay packet from the pit with paper money in it, instead of gold half sovereigns and coppers.' She had a tear in her eye; then she went on to say, 'He took the paper notes out and the coppers and tore the packet up, threw it on the fire and said, 'God's cuss. Them and their fake money.' Aye, and I remember our Maisy writing to that soldier in the trenches in 1917 and all of us in Mrs McNamee's class knitting woollen socks for the poor soldiers in the trenches as well.'

Mrs Minogue pipes up again, 'Aye, well I was only nine, but I was a great reader and writer for me age. Mrs McNamee asked the older children to write to the troops to cheer them up and because I was a good writer she let me send a letter as well. The letters came back answered and addressed to St Patrick's School with our names on them. I remember how delighted we all were to get letters back.

'I don't know what I said in my letter to confuse the poor soldier. I remember sending him his socks and five Woodbines and a letter. He wrote back and thanked me for the fags and socks and asked if he could go out with me when he was next on leave.' She was giggling like a drain now, fully back to her old self. She said, 'Daddy, Lord rest him, went bloody mad and said, "He must think you're fourteen, the poor bugger. You'd better write back and tell him he can't go out with you, you're only nine, then finish with the letter writing, do you hear me?" I was always getting into trouble,' she said.

Well, I don't know about getting into trouble, but somehow Mrs Minogue had made me see how different life was in her younger days from what life was like for me. They were used to death, what with TB and wars; Catholics and Protestants hating each other; having to leave Cleator Moor to find work, being discriminated against and afraid of being attacked on the way home from school. They were hardened to life's hard ways.

Maybe that was why they were accepting the death of poor Cuthy. They were conditioned to take these shocks and tragedies and to cope with them. Their generation was better prepared for disaster than mine was. I'd never known hunger or any form of hardship for that matter, and children and young people just don't die now. At least not on Cleator Moor. So somehow her stories seemed to put things into some sort of perspective and I was more able to accept the death of our young friend because of this experience, and Mrs Minogue.

CHAPTER 4
DAD'S BIT OF PSYCHOLOGY WORKED

Dad and Uncle Eddie have recently sold our beach bungalow at Nethertown. It's been a bit of a sad time because we've spent the last ten years holidaying at Nethertown, spending weeks and weeks at a time in the asbestos shelter we called a bungalow. Papa Heron, Dad and Uncle Eddie Devoy built the bungalow in the early 1950s for all the family to use. Our two families and Auntie Lily's used it mostly during the main summer holidays. It was rented out to neighbours and friends for the rest of the summer months, but of late the lion's share of the maintenance has been done by Dad because Papa's too old and Uncle Eddie is too badly; he's hardly able to sit in the bar of the Millers Inn, of which he and Auntie Winnie (Mam's sister) are the tenants.

The bungalow needed a lot of attention this spring because the winter storms have caused a lot of damage. One of the shutters was blown off one of the big windows under the front veranda and the storm blew the window in and caused a lot of water damage to furniture and carpets. Dad has made good the damage and replaced the carpets, but even worse news arrived this week from the farmer who owns the land the bungalow is built on; he wants to sell the land. Up-to-date, we've paid an annual ground rent for the bungalow to the farmer and the periodical rents have more than covered the cost of the ground rent and maintenance, but £300 is going to take a lot of finding, so I think that has been the final straw.

I suppose it's time to move on. Maybe in future we'll go further afield for our holidays, but it heralds the end of an era for our family and that brings its regrets. I'm thinking these thoughts while lying in bed on a Saturday morning; a thing I seldom do, but this morning I've got no special reason to get up. It's about nine o'clock, Stephen is in the double bed, Barry has gone to cricket practice (he's home on holiday from the Junior Seminary) and Dad's doing his window round.

The bedroom window's open and I can hear Dad's voice talking to a neighbour. She says, 'Good morning, Mr Close. It's a lovely day, isn't it?'

And Dad answers, 'It is, lass. I'll get some windows cleaned today, lass, with a good wind behind me.' Then Dad says, 'By the way, you wouldn't happen to have seen a pair of cricket boots lying around anywhere have you?'

And she replies, 'No, I haven't, Mr Close. Why, have you lost a pair?'

To which Dad replies, 'Well, put it this way, they've gone missing off the washing line. Our Barry whitened them and hung them by the laces onto the line to dry and they've gone missing.'

'Well, I'll keep an eye open for them, Mr Close,' she says.

'Aye, well if they turn up before the day's out I won't need to go to the police,' says Dad, and moves his ladder onto the next house.

Our Barry had a mania for keeping his cricket whites and boots clean. The boots had been a present from Uncle Robbie (Dad's brother), one of many presents bestowed on Barry during his stay at the Junior Seminary. I suppose people thought they would spoil him with gifts because he was separated from the family for much of his time. Stephen, Margaret and I understood this and didn't mind him being indulged when he was at home. Besides, we didn't like cricket anyway. By the way, the boots turned up on the back step later in the day, returned by persons unknown. So, the matter was taken no further.

I could get up and take my young cousins, Geraldine and Diane (they're only two and four) for a ride round the fell road on my bike. I've fitted a child's seat to the back for this very purpose; or I could cut the grass, which Dad's neglecting this morning for his window round; or I could go down to Dad's hen garden and take a look at the day-old chicks, see how they're getting on. They're lovely to watch with the old mother hen fussing about with them, keeping them out of harm's way.

Or, alternatively, I could just lie here and do nowt: that's the beauty of Saturday mornings. Mam says I should take the good of them because in less than a year I'll be working full-time and, likely as not, working Saturday mornings. No, I think I'll just enjoy perfect peace and quiet and let the day unwind in its own good time.

I finally get up and opt for a stroll down to the hen garden where Dad keeps a huge hut full of hens producing dozens of eggs every day. He uses the deep litter method which requires the hens to be locked up all the time in the hut. The deep litter is a mixture of peat and organic material to a depth of about six inches in the bottom of the hut. The hens can scratch in this and are fed directly onto the deep litter as well as feeding troughs.

This is supposed to be a more natural alternative to keeping them locked up in cages. They have nesting boxes to lay the eggs in all around the hut walls which can be emptied from a lid on the outside of the hut. The hens can roost on wooden poles across the centre of the hut and they seem quite happy. He also keeps a few free range hens for our own private eggs, and some ducks he's fattening up for Christmas.

The ground round the hen huts is like a padding can, grassless and muddy from years of constant treading from the various poultry. Dad doesn't like killing the badly hens, or the fat ducks, so, usually, he calls in Uncle Faley. He has his own method of humanely killing the birds. I've seen him do it; in fact I've often helped him. He places the hens or ducks head on a wooden block and puts a steel pole over their neck. Then he applies pressure on both sides of the steel pole 'til the bird breathes no more. This only takes seconds and doesn't seem to hurt the birds. He says it's less cruel than wringing their necks.

Today, however, no such activity is taking place. The ducks are swimming in the man-made pool at the bottom of the garden and the day-old chicks are following their mother round the garden like a troupe of Spanish dancers while she pecks at the grassless earth, and I just feel so lucky to be alive.

I'll just sit in the warm sunshine on the bench made of old railway sleepers and smell the strong scent of creosote emanating from them. I let my mind drift away to a land of prairie grasses and tumble weed. To the Mississippi and the world of Tom Sawyer and Huckleberry Finn. The warm breeze and the strong scent of creosote soon knocks me out and I sleep the sleep of an innocent child, soon to be wakened by a boulder scopped into the duck pond by Malcolm Tate soaking me to the skin.

This is probably the last time I'll ever have such complete peace of mind for a very long time.

CHAPTER 5
SAINT CUTHBERT'S SCHOOL

My introduction to secondary school, Saint Cuthbert's RC Secondary Modern, as it was known, took place on 2nd September 1959. I walked the five minute walk from Seaview Place with my twin brother Stephen, both resplendent in our new school uniforms – black pants, black blazer, school badge, white shirt and yellow and orange striped tie. We'd had our hair cut in a modest, not too short crew cut by Dad on the back step of our house the day before. My ear was still stinging where he'd caught it with the clippers.

The bright, still morning had the first hint of autumn about it and my heart was in my mouth. There was a light procession of new intakes similarly clad in our slightly too large jackets which would have to last at least a full year. I felt rather awkward because the sleeves were a bit long and I had to keep my arms bent to give the impression that the jacket fitted. I knew a good few of my fellow pupils because they lived round and about me, but many of the faces were new.

The anticipation was awesome. Stephen and me chatted and joked with some of our would-be classmates. We feigned a convincing bravado, but deep down I was less than confident. Like most children of my age, I was making the monumental leap from a small junior school to what seemed like a massive secondary school, and I wasn't convinced I was fully capable of it. However, my thirst for new friends and acquaintances would be my salvation.

The large numbers of students and apparent vastness of the school with its long corridors and two flights of stairs, was somewhat reassuring. I felt I could maintain my anonymity and become invisible among the throng. Not so. Like a military operation, we were herded into our predetermined streamed classes. Stephen and me were deposited into class 1A. The streaming was determined by your 11+ result and Steve and me, to our surprise, had just failed a pass to the grammar school, so we were placed in the A form. What a coup! It had a certain kudos to be an A-former.

Our form teacher, Miss Cunningham, nickname Drac (short for

Count Dracula), proved to be equal to her namesake. She introduced herself by writing her name on the blackboard: 'Miss Cunningham'. She went on to explain that her name could be broken down into two words: 'cunning' and 'ham'. Cunning being self explanatory, and Ham, a question, 'which animal do we get ham from?' The question, being unanswered, was repeated and an answer demanded.

The answer was provided by Martin Foley. 'A pig, Miss!'.

'Yes,' said Miss Cunningham. She then wrote on the blackboard the words 'cunning pig'. 'You will do well to remember these two words. I will be told of your every move and woe betide any one of you who steps out of line or crosses me. I'm the one you will be answerable to, and I don't like first-years.'

This had the desired effect of crushing most of us, myself included. Drac had established her ground rules in the first few seconds of our first lesson. This was to be her 'tour-de-force'. She then lightened up a bit and said she would make a better friend than enemy and as long as we toed the line we should get on fine. That was as light as she ever got.

She was one for analysing names and was most amused by my name, Sean Close. She change it to 'Shaven Closely' and used it on me on many occasions, much to my embarrassment. Thankfully, we would have no more than two lessons a day from Drac, registration being one of them, so surely the rest of our teachers wouldn't be as bad as her! Quite so. We had some very good, kind people to guide us through our adolescent years and for whom I had the greatest respect.

The religious zealotry of most of my teachers manifested itself to different degrees, all of them reaffirming the strong Catholic ethos of the school, in the best tradition of 'Little Ireland'.

Our school day always started with assembly. The whole school in the main hall with seasonal hymns and prayers to the Saints of the day, with special emphasis on Saint Patrick, Saint Cuthbert, our school patron and Our Lady of Lourdes.

The Catholic church has a very neat calendar of devotions throughout the year, dedicating certain times and whole months to certain themes. October, for instance, is dedicated to Our Lady with the October devotions. November is dedicated to the Holy Souls.

Prayers are offered for the recently and not so recently dead throughout the month. 'Waste not in selfish weeping one precious day, for the souls in their still agony, good Christians pray', as one of the popular November hymns says.

December, of course, was Advent – the preparation for the birth of Jesus and a time for reflection and anticipation. We were not encouraged to be swept along on the tide of commercialism which was fast taking over from the real reason to celebrate Christmas, although we did have our Christmas party, and the joy of a good dance and merry-making was encouraged, but that was secondary to the joy of the holy season.

March meant lent for six weeks, no sweets or weekly treats. April was usually Easter and the solemnity of the Crucifixion and death of Christ. Then the Glorious Resurrection was very much hammered home to us. May followed with the mood changing to the joyful hymn-singing devoted once again to Our Lady, decorating her statues with May flowers.

The assembly was also used as a platform for the Headmaster to make important announcements, reminders of the Holy days of obligation for the coming week and mentioning any particular problems involving bad behaviour of pupils and his proposed regime to eradicate these problems.

One such problem springs to mind, and concerns the illegal practice of lads smoking in the toilets. Mr Paterson had mounted a campaign, with the help of prefects, to catch the culprits and make an example of them in front of the whole school. He'd managed to acquire four names to inflict his ordeal by fire on (or should I say ordeal by smoke). He called the names out during morning assembly, and told the lads, all fourth formers, to step up onto the stage.

The boys did this in a very belligerent manner and approached Mr Paterson without any apparent fear. He then asked then in turn if, in fact, they had been smoking in the toilets and did they know this was against school rules. To which they all answered 'Yes' to both questions. Mr Paterson then went on, with a trace of sarcasm in his tone, asking the boys if they enjoyed smoking, to which they again unanimously replied 'Yes, Sir'.

Mr Paterson then produced a packet of Senior Service and proceeded to light one. He then said to the lads, who seemed to be enjoying their new-found notoriety and who were moving about on the stage in a rather provocative manner, 'Would you care for a smoke?' The boys were not quite sure how serious a question this was at first and didn't answer, but when Mr Paterson offered each one of them in turn a cigarette they all took one from him. He then lit their cigarettes and instructed them to start smoking.

He turned back round to the assembly and told us his theory, whereby if the lads were made to smoke until they were sick, they would never touch a cigarette again. He was about to be made a complete fool of and his theory shot down literally in flames. The boys meanwhile continued enjoying their fags. To fill in the time, Mr Paterson smoked his own cigarette and produced a large white hankie from his top pocket and held it up to his face.

By this time I was convinced that he'd either pull a white dove or a rabbit from his hankie, just like David Nixon does on the telly, but no, nothing so entertaining. Mind you, we were being well entertained by the lads behind him who were all blowing smoke circles and trying to see who could make the biggest ring.

Mr Paterson gave a very convincing demonstration on how smoking can harm our lungs. He inhaled a huge amount of smoke and blew it through his white handkerchief. This left a very large and visible brown mark. 'That is what is left in our lungs every time we inhale a cigarette,' he said. 'So imagine how that can eventually clog the lungs and cause untold harm to your health,' he said.

I was totally convinced by now, never to take a single drag from another fag for the rest of my life. I did, however, wonder how he could justify this condemnation of the dreaded weed and still continue to smoke like a chimney himself, as did many of the teaching staff. This was very evident when you looked into the staff room at playtimes and saw the teachers disappearing through the staff room door into a total blackout of cigarette smoke.

By now, the lads had finished their first fag and getting stuck into their second one gaining more confidence and displaying more truculence by the minute. The other members of staff, some of whom were on the stage and some on door duty, were beginning to look decidedly uncomfortable. The lads however, after another few fags and an empty packet in Mr Pattinsons hands, were showing no sign of slowing down or feeling sick for that matter.

Mr Pattinson, like the true trooper that he was, was not prepared to lose face completely and declared, 'Due to lack of cigarettes, this experiment has to be discontinued, but had it continued much longer, I am sure the lads would all throw up on the stage. For that reason the boys can leave the stage and go to my office, where they will be dealt six of the best.'

I don't remember Mr Pattinson staging any other similar stunts for the remainder of his reign as head. The lads, on the other hand, went on to engage in criminal activities, and one of them was expelled for an accumulation of reasons, not just the smoking escapade.

Smoking in the toilets resumed after a few weeks and the status quo was re-established. Pupil power was emerging as a force to be reckoned with.

CHAPTER 6
ELVIO MANGO

I had been at Saint Cuthbert's for about two terms or so when two new pupils arrived mid-term and proved to be quite a curiosity. They were Italian. Their names were Angelo and Elvio Mango. Elvio was a first-year and couldn't speak a single word of English. Angelo was older, very tall, dark and moody-looking. All the lasses were round him like bees on a jam jar. Elvio was introduced by Mr Tool, our English teacher (nickname Penman) to our class and we were told he would need special treatment and help from the whole class, because he couldn't speak any English. Poor Elvio was stood beside Penman like a spare priest at a wedding, obviously completely unable to understand what was going on or what was being said.

Penman announced that Sean and Stephen Close had been chosen to take him under their wing for a settling-in period and we would be responsible for watching him during playtimes and lesson changes. (It would have been nice to have been asked if we didn't mind.) This responsibility proved one hell of a challenge, because Elvio, it turned out, would be taking full advantage of his lack of English, especially when it suited him not to understand. He was placed next to me and Stephen was moved to the next bench with Peter McDowell. Elvio wasn't given any special English lessons during school hours. He may have had tuition after school, I don't know. He was a terrible distraction during lessons because he wouldn't sit still and he spoke out in Italian any time he decided he wanted to, regardless of whether we were all working or the teachers were talking.

Some of the teachers tolerated this behaviour and encouraged him with things they thought him capable of, but some of them sent him out of the class if he persisted in being disruptive. That meant that either Stephen or me had to accompany him, and as soon as we got out of our classroom he was off like a gazelle, down the corridor from 1A form room with me in hot pursuit. He'd barge into the woodwork room without knocking, and me after him trying to haul him out by his arm back into the main corridor. Pop Worsley, the woodwork teacher, threw a lump of wood at us one day and told us to knock before we entered his classroom; but of course

Elvio didn't understand. (Or did he?)

I'm not sure if he was really thick or really clever. He was in a unique position; nobody really knew how much he could understand, and nearly always gave him the benefit of the doubt. I was rather surprised how much better behaved and more sociable his older brother Angelo seemed to be, and how much better his English was; and whenever we encountered Angelo in the school corridor he always seemed to scream and shout at Elvio in Italian. I think Elvio was milking his lack of English for all it was worth.

That particular summer we were having some really good weather. Good enough to persuade Mam to let us camp out down the mill, which was a deep pool in the curve of the beck (Hen Beck) near the Kangol factory and the paper mill at Brookside. We were allowed to pitch our tent by the back edge of the far bank away from the factory yards from Friday night until Sunday night inclusive by some unwritten law, according to local legend.

So we would set of after school and, after a good meal on Mam's insistence and on condition that we came home on Sunday morning, got washed and changed and went to ten o'clock Mass then changed back into our camping gear (Khaki shorts and T-shirts) to continue our camp for the rest of Sunday.

The logistics of this would seem complicated to anybody who isn't familiar with Cleator Moor, but in fact, this whole weekend activity was taking place within a quarter of a mile of our house. So the Sunday Mass ritual was no real problem. Mam was even prepared to bring Sunday dinner forward to half-past eleven, so we would have a good meal and have the rest of the day camping. (She'd get a whole weekend of peace and quiet out of it as well.) We set off, Stephen, me and a cuddy-load of bread, tins of beans and sausage, a couple of pints of milk and eggs and bacon.

We had a brand-new nylon four-berth tent, complete with canvas ground sheet and blankets. We'd be as snug as a bug in a rug, Mam said. We'd have to rely on fallen branches for our camp fire, but there was no shortage of them at the Mill. To get to the far bank meant crossing the beck at the shallows, and when you get to the other side, you feel as if you were miles away on some deserted tropical island, except that, because of the heatwave, everybody and their dog had the same idea and the place was like Butlin's holiday camp.

Dad had bought the new tent with Embassy cigarette coupons. He smoked that many cigarettes he could have kitted out the whole Cleator Moor number two section scout troop and still have enough left for a three-piece suite! So why he didn't get the separate waterproof fly sheet to go with the tent I'll never know. We hadn't expected rain, and when it came in the night we weren't quite prepared for the deluge of drips that penetrated the new tent roof and walls.

We were first aware that all was not well when I felt what seemed like a slight mist inside the tent just after the rain started as we were climbing into our home-made sleeping bags – a woollen blanket folded double and pinned together on the open side with a thousand safety pins. The instructions that came with the tent assured us that the tent was fully shower-proof, but suggested the extra waterproof fly sheet that went over the tent and was an optional extra would only be necessary in very inclement conditions. Dad had decided he'd save some coupons and hope for the best, so didn't order the fly sheet. This was to be our undoing. The instructions had also said to avoid touching the inside walls of the tent in wet weather, as this could encourage a slight drip at the point of contact. I mean, why didn't we smell a rat? Poor Dad had been sold a pup and practically smoked himself into oblivion in the process.

When somebody tells you not to do something because something will happen when you do, you can't resist doing it to see if it is true. Stephen pushed the palm of his hand on the tent wall just above his head, and he might as well have been lying under the Lodore Falls. Within ten seconds the water was dripping onto his face and he jumped up out of his sleeping blanket and rubbed his back against the whole of his side of the tent wall. We spent all the rest of the night cramped top to tail in my sleeping blanket and trying to divert the torrents of water which were racing through the tent on Stephen's side. We just opened the zip at the front of the tent and let the water flow out.

Despite having to suffer Stephen's big toe up my nose for most of the night. I managed to sleep and so did Stephen. Mind you, he could sleep on a clothes-line. His big problem isn't sleeping, it's waking up. Mam shouts us all up for school together. Barry and Margaret and me wake normally and take it in turns to use the bathroom. It's usually a race between us three to get to the bathroom first. Not Stephen. He doesn't enter into this contest. He staggers out of bed, floats downstairs, half comatose and continues his sleep for at least a quarter of an hour on the settee in the living room, by which time the rest of us have washed, cleaned our teeth and had our breakfasts. Stephen then has sole access to all the facilities from there on in, and somehow manages to catch up with the rest of us, with a lot of help from Mam.

The morning arrived, as it inevitably does, in a blaze of sunlight streaming through the white sodden walls of our tent, making the atmosphere feel like a Chinese laundry. I woke first (wouldn't you know?) and stretched my arms free of the damp sleeping blanket. I crawled out of the tent in my underpants and paddled round the side of the tent for a pee. If you need a big job you have to discreetly stroll into the woods and find a convenient tree amongst some low undergrowth to do the necessary, keeping an eye out for nettles.

I could see the factory workers arriving for their Saturday morning shift and felt lucky to be free of any such encumbrance. I couldn't light a fire because all the dead wood was too wet to burn, so I settled for a plate of cold sausage and beans and a drink of milk. I felt cheated out of my bacon and eggs, but that's all part of the unpredictability of camping. Stephen eventually emerged from his state of stupor and the day began. After mopping up inside the tent and hanging our blankets over a fallen tree trunk to dry we set off to engage in the sport of the day, namely the swing over the beck. Some other campers joined in this exercise and the morning drifted towards noon.

Our New Best Friend

Our new best friend and charge, Elvio, mysteriously arrived about mid-day, just as we were preparing to light our camp fire and frustrated our attempts by piling loads of wet leaves onto the already struggling flames. This had the effect of completely extinguishing the fire and caused Stephen to chase him threatening to throttle him if he came anywhere near the tent again. This of course he ignored, pleading non-comprehendo. Somehow Elvio had claimed international immunity in the event of every misdemeanour, but our patience was wearing thin.

He continued to disrupt our afternoon's game by commandeering the swing when he felt like it. He didn't understand the principle of taking turns and made himself very unpopular with everybody who was swimming in the beck by deliberately splashing everybody within ten feet of the river bank, whether or not they were wearing swimming trunks. His most serious prank he kept in reserve until the beck and the bank were full of afternoon revellers, when he removed all his clothes and jumped into the beck bollock-naked.

The lasses all screamed, pretending to be shocked, and one group of three lasses clambered out of the water and ran to hide in their tent, which was just a few yards from ours. Stephen and me had intended to get to know these three lasses a bit better and had been engaged in some horse-play with them in the water when Elvio started his master stroke of attention-seeking. As soon as he saw the lasses running into the tent he shot off out of the water and ran in after them.

He was extremely unselfconscious about his nakedness and emerged several times running round the tent shouting excitedly at the crowd who had gathered to witness this strange event. The lasses meanwhile were obviously distressed by his antics and Stephen and me rushed over to the tent, by which time Elvio was back inside, throwing himself on top of the lasses and making terrible animal-like noises.

We managed to drag him off the lasses and out of the tent and Stephen smacked him one on the nose-end. He didn't retaliate, he just screamed as if he were in terrible pain and dashed over to the bank to retrieve his clothes. He dressed on the hoof and disappeared from sight amid shouts of abuse from the bathers.

We were the heroes of the day and the lasses in the tent, after recovering from the shock, played up to us and gave us sandwiches and cakes and sweets and gave us a very good time for the rest of the afternoon. Elvio had done us a favour, really. We might not have made such good headway without his help.

CHAPTER 7
OLD RELICS

I must say this religion thing is starting to wear a bit thin. Mam's been dragging me off to the Novena to Saint Philomena every night this week. I've looked up in the Lives of the Saints. She was a child martyr who lived in the third century, and she is the patron saint of children. She's a great favourite of Mam's and in fact her popularity has reached cult proportions. Churches, schools and shrines to the saint have sprung up all over the country.

This Novena (Novena means nine days' prayer) is to be the last ever Novena to the saint at Saint Mary's Church, because Pope John has given her the axe, declaring the evidence to support this saint as too sparse, and so she is being removed from the liturgical calendar. Mam's devastated. She's a member of the Saint Philomena Society and can't understand why the Pope sees fit to sack the saint, though the Novena will culminate in the veneration of the saint's relic, which Saint Mary's has treasured for years.

I've seen the saint's relic and it's a piece of bone which is supposed to have come from her actual body. Father McCann carries the relic above his head all around the church and it's held in a silver case covered with a blue velvet cloth during the veneration service. The relic is then placed on the altar rails and the congregation is invited to kiss the relic. Well, not the actual relic, just the case. You can see through the glass front of the relic case what looks like a bad tooth. I don't fancy kissing that. It's been around for seventeen hundred years. God love it, it deserves to be buried, not stared at like some item in a freak show.

I wonder where Father McCann got the relic from. Maybe you can get them from ancient relics catalogues like Great Universal or Littlewoods. I'm sure we had other relics at Saint Mary's. I remember a few years ago going to a service to see a saint's relic, which was on tour (relics must have been like latter-day pop stars). I think it was a part of Padre Peah's habit. He's not actually a saint yet because he's still alive, but he will be some day. Anyhow, the church was full that night and people were hoping the relic would cure them of sickness. Padre Peah has the stigmata, which are the wounds of Christ in his hands and side. They weep blood and won't heal up. He's a really holy man.

We're in the midst of big changes in the Catholic Church. Soon we're going to be able to eat meat on Fridays, except for Good Friday. Dad says Coles' wet fish shop on the Moor will go out of business. We're not going to have to fast from the night before we take communion on Sundays any more. I think that's a good idea, because I'm famished on Sunday mornings, having no breakfast till we get back from nine o'clock Mass. I swallow my bacon and eggs without them even touching the sides. It's not going to be the same, Dad says. No pain, no gain.

They seem to be doing away with penance altogether. Women are going to be able to go to church without having to wear a hat, and just as the mantilla is becoming the new fashion accessory! (Bad news for the millinery industry.) People will stick to the old ways for a long time. I can't see the Mortan sisters giving up their hats without a fight.

The biggest change is going to be having the Mass in English. We're losing the old Latin mass and a lot of people don't agree with that. We'll have to learn the responses in English and the congregation will have to make the responses instead of the altar boys. That should keep some of the old-timers awake. You often see old people at the back of the church during Mass snoring their heads off. That's all going to stop. And standing outside having a smoke during Mass will have to stop. Mind you, I don't think that has ever really been allowed, but loads of the young lads do that at Cleator. They might as well stay at home. I mean, what do they get out of it?

Aunty May says how is she going to get her rosary said if she's going to be interrupted every five minutes with having to say responses. I've watched her at Mass. She goes into a trance, with her rosary beads clicking fifty to the dozen like a horse in full gallop on cobble stones. The likes of Aunty May will never hack these changes, they're too old. The Mass to them is a time to meditate, and they do. You can hear them whispering the rosary and their private prayers.

One old lady who sits at the back of the church, when I've arrived late sometimes I've squeezed in beside her, has a proper crack with God. I think she's deaf and she can't hear her own voice. She says things like, 'Dear God, my almighty saviour, please help our Agnes to get her wee problem, you know what I mean, sorted out. She's nearly demented, and Mammy's stopped wearing her teeth and can only manage beef tea. Please make her put her teeth in for us, and get a proper meal into her. God help her, she's skin and bone, and I know it's a lot to ask, but can you see yourself clear to letting me lose a couple of stone, I'm struggling to get meself to Holy Mass with me feet and I can hardly get me coat buttoned up. Only if you see fit, my dear God in Heaven.' I mean, how is she going to be able to have a proper crack with God and concentrate on the English responses at the same time? It can't be done. I think some of them will just stop going to Mass altogether, saying they can't manage the walk any more. Mind you, it will be nice to see the lasses' bare heads and long flowing locks.

Mam says things have to change to keep pace with modern life. Young people just won't keep these things going, so they're best let go of now, before they're rejected without the permission of the Pope. Things have been the same in the Catholic church for such a long time, but there must have been other times in history when the church had to make drastic changes, and they no doubt would have been met with mistrust. I wish they would get shot of Confession. That would be a great help to me. But I haven't heard of that being a possibility. Well, not yet, anyway.

CHAPTER 8
THE BIRDS AND THE BEES
AND THE CIGARETTE TREES

Sex education lessons were not top of the agenda at Saint Cuthbert's. 'Keep them in the dark and maybe they won't bother' was more like the official line. Sex was looked upon as something dirty and not to be encouraged or talked about. The nearest to a sex education lesson we ever had (unless I was off that day) was from the big sulky red-faced priest who descended upon us at the beginning of the second year.

Mr Pattinson announced from the stage during assembly one morning that all second year boys from 2A, 2B and 2C should remain in the Hall after assembly for a talk by Father Damian, a visiting Cistercian Monk. This priest's greatest skill as a lecturer was in completing the whole forty-five minute lesson without mentioning the words 'sex', 'erection', 'penis' or 'masturbation'. The lesson, in fact, wasn't to give us any guidance on sexual matters at all, but to reaffirm the doctrine that the practice of masturbation is a mortal sin. That's the last thing you want to hear when your hormones are doing somersaults and astrakhan rugs are appearing in your Y-fronts and under your arms as we speak.

The grim reaper spoke about waking up during the night feeling peculiar (maybe that was his word for 'erection'), having a strange sensation and discomfort (still no sign of a penis). If we experience this sensation we should close our eyes and go back to sleep. We shouldn't touch ourselves (still no mention of penis). If that didn't work and we still felt peculiar we should think of nuns! (what?), the purity of nuns, and say a prayer to Our Lady.

Well, for God's sake, that was some tall order. Surely our wet dreams are our own business and our only legitimate way of sexual release? Apparently not. They've got the whole sex thing sown up. I don't know how Catholics ever manage to procreate without committing suicide immediately after the sordid act. We're all sent on this terrible guilt trip.

Well, the grim reaper went down like a fart in a wet suit with the lads. We were dismissed by Father Peculiar (sorry, Father Damian, his name was quite apt really) and left the Hall with our tails between our legs, so to speak. As soon as the last lad stepped into the corridor and closed the door behind him, we all erupted in the loudest roar of laughter the school had ever heard. Peculiar, my arse!

The One-Eyed Monster

I had, of course, by now discovered the dual purpose of my penis. It was no longer only a means by which to pee, but was the source of extreme pleasure and entertainment. I had discovered masturbation; and once discovered, there was no going back. I won't dwell on this adolescent preoccupation, because every teenage lad experiences it. It's good practice for the real thing. In fact, it's a wonderful aside in its own right.

My dalliance in self-gratification was seriously marred by the fact that I knew it was a mortal sin to spill the seed except for the purposes of procreation, and only allowed in the marital situation by proclamation of the Catholic church. For some strange reason, this made it all the more exciting. The forbidden fruits and all that. But this left me with a terrible battle with my conscience, and hung over me (forgive the pun) like the sword of Damocles.

This became a battle of wills between my confessors, who for the most part forbade the practices, except for Father O'Connell, who told me not to think too deeply about it and to restrict it to the occasions when I couldn't help myself. That advice only served to confuse me further, because I could never help myself. The demons in my head take over, and when the sap rises the Bishop gets another bashing.

I'd often thought about not mentioning the one-eyed monster in confession and adding an extra couple of Hail Marys to my penance, but what would have been the point? I would only have been fooling myself, because God knows everything. If things get too bad I could cut out the middle man and stop going to confession altogether and just make a good act of contrition, but I wouldn't get the grace from the sacrament of confession and I'd never be able to fight the devil on my own.

I have to be truthful in confession or it would get to the point where I would allow myself to commit the most heinous sins in the world and only confess to kicking the cat. That wouldn't make it alright. It's all such a bother. The visitations from the devil in the night are the best, because I have no control over them. I just wake up in a wet patch and feel no guilt.

CHAPTER 9
PRIVY TO TOO MUCH INFORMATION
THE DEVIL FINDS WORK FOR IDLE HANDS

All through my childhood and adolescence I have taken in, sometimes on a subconscious level, information which was not actually stated, merely hinted at. I was a perceptive, yet naïve child. During my period of serving Mass I was privy to many of the idiosyncrasies and personal habits of the priests I served Mass for.

I must point out at this point that Cleator Parish was one of the biggest parishes in the Lancaster Diocese, mostly because of Cleator Moor's large number per head of population of Irish Catholics. The parish was considered to be a wealthy parish, well financed by the generous and well-attending parishioners who flocked to the many Sunday Masses. Five Masses were said on Sundays and two daily. At some of the Masses it was literally standing room only if you didn't get to your seat at least a quarter of an hour before Mass started. So because of this, Father McCann, the parish priest, often had upwards of half a dozen priests in residence at any one time.

Because of the nature of the parish and its ability to accommodate a lot of priests, a few of the priests in residence were sent to Cleator to recuperate from problems they may have had, and could be absorbed, if only to say some of the many Masses, both weekly and daily. Some of the priests, not all of course, were social misfits, some with drink problems. This was not a well broadcast fact, but my perception as a young altar boy soon sussed them out.

One priest, I remember, regularly said half past seven Mass in the morning during the week, and when my turn for serving his Mass turned up on the serving rota I was always on my guard. He had a habit of sleeping on the chair in the vestry. At least, he was always asleep on the chair when I arrived at a quarter past seven. Whether he had been there all night or not I really don't know, but he always smelt of drink and I had to waken him up and tell him it was time for Mass.

He was never best pleased to be wakened and I used to step back after prodding him for fear of a lurch or verbal abuse. He would stagger about and often needed help to get into his vestments. He was always able to say Mass and to administer the sacraments, but there was no interaction between any of the servers; we just did our duty and never spoke about it to anyone. We respected his ministry and did our duty; it was not our place to judge. A lot of the priests were very distant and seemed almost unaware of the presence of the altar servers. I put this down to their spirituality and the fact that they needed their own space to psyche themselves up to prepare themselves for saying Mass. The priest said various prayers while putting on his vestments and we kept very much in the background.

One such priest was a young man, probably only in his late twenties. I served his Mass regularly and he always treated me with indifference, until after a few weeks of serving his Mass, he'd finished putting his vestments away and I was about to go to school after placing my surplice on the hanger in the servers' wardrobe. He approached me with a letter he was holding and addressed me by my name, a thing he'd never done before. He asked me if I could do him a favour and deliver a letter for him to an address in Fletcher Street. I said, 'Of course, Father,' and took the letter from him. He asked me to be careful and put the letter in the right letter box because he didn't want it to get into the wrong hands. I agreed with enthusiasm and assured him I'd be certain to deliver it to the address on the envelope.

This practice continued for some weeks, maybe once or twice a week, and I noticed it was always me he gave the envelope to. For some reason I'd forgotten to deliver a letter, and when my mother found it in my blazer pocket she asked me who had given it to me. When I told her the priest's name she told me never to take any more letters from him and said Dad would be giving the letter to Father McCann. She asked me how many times I'd delivered letters for the priest, and I told her and asked her what the mystery was. She said the woman was a prostitute and I wasn't to ask any more questions about it, but I wasn't to deliver any more messages for the priest, and if he asked me I was to say my Dad says I haven't to deliver your letters any more.

Needless to say, he never did ask me and he treated me with his usual indifference, but didn't remain at Cleator for very long afterwards. I didn't ask any questions of Mam and Dad on this subject, I knew the least said, the sooner mended was the order of the day.

CHAPTER 10
OBSESSIVE BEHAVIOUR

This period in my life could be described as my obsessive period. For some strange reason I found myself counting everything in sight. For instance, lamp posts and gate stoops were two of my obsessions. The point of the exercise as I saw it was to finish counting on an even number. Ten was a good number, or fifty, or better still, one hundred. Thirty wasn't bad, but not as good as fifty or sixty.

Gable ends was another, because you could count five points to a gable end and if you passed ten houses you got fifty points. Sometimes a gate stoop would be missing and that would knock me off course, so I'd have to continue counting until I found another gate with a missing stoop. Gable ends could be a problem, because some people built extensions to their houses and the gable ends would change shape, leaving a very bad number of points: six, in itself not such a bad number because it was at least even, but difficult to make a ten out of it. I mean, you never get a gable end with four points, so I had to innovate and count a couple of gate stoops in to get me back on track.

Steps was another. I hated uneven numbers of steps. When I was delivering the Universe on Crag Road and New Todholes Road I could count over a hundred steps in total, but as soon as I reached a hundred I stopped counting them and started on paving stones. These were easy, because you could miss out the odd one and end up on an even number. Our stairs in Seaview Place were a great source of consolation, because there were twelve of them and that was a really good number for some reason.

My preoccupation with counting extended to lines left by the lawn mower. Dad was a keen gardener, at least, keen on growing vegetables. He had a wee greenhouse he'd made from old window frames and he grew tomatoes and lettuce, and when they were finished he grew late chrysanthemums. The only trouble was the lawns; he hated cutting them. Because I showed an interest in gardening this became my job. Cutting the grass every week in summer I enjoyed because it was a precise art. At least, I made it one. The problem was the shape of the back lawn. It wasn't a square, it was more of a triangle with a square end and to get a complete line on the angle with the lawn mower was impossible. I did find a way round it, though. I made sure the last three lines left by the mower measured up to one complete line, the same length as the others. Well, more or less. But I had to organise my cutting very carefully.

This period tailed off a bit after a year or so and I was able to cross the market square without even looking at the lamp posts. I decided it wasn't worth the trouble. I don't think I ever told a soul about it. I think I got it from Mam, because she was one for working to a routine. She had to clean the windows at least once a week and the house was always sparkling and clean. Every surface polished and sparkling clean. Mind you, we soon made it dirty again and she didn't make us feel uncomfortable, because she always maintained a house was to be lived in, but she never let things slide.

Dad certainly wasn't obsessed with tidiness, or anything else for that matter. He never knew where to find a thing. Mam says he leaves everything at his backside for her to clean up. He was always promising to sort things out, and Mam would say, 'Yes, Jay, when Nelson gets his eye back.'

CHAPTER 11
JAY AND EDDY DRINK DRIVING

It was funny the other day when Aunty Winnie came round. She said to Mam, 'What do you make of them two eejits?'

And Mam said, 'Who do you mean, Winnie?'

And she said, 'Jay and Eddy, who do you think I mean?'

Eddy was Aunty Winnie's husband and Dad's best friend, his drinking partner. Winnie went on, 'Well, they both fell through the door at half past twelve on Saturday night, drunk as skunks. I said, "My God, what a state to come home in, the pair of yous." And Jay, you know what he's like in drink, Eileen, he says, "Oh, now, come on, Winnie, lass, we've had a real good night, Eddy and me, so don't you go and spoil it for us, fussing and facing", and then set off laughing. I said, "How have you got home?" And Eddy says, "Jay brought me home in the car". '

Winnie said 'Have you been driving that car in your state?'

And Dad said, 'Well, now, I couldn't see Eddy making his way home in this (meaning the weather) so I got the old Rover out and brought him home.'

Now, by this time Dad was falling all over the place so Eddy insisted on driving him back home in the old Rover.

Eddy had said, 'I'll take him home, lass, he's not walking home in this, as sure as there's an eye in a goat.'

Winnie said 'I told them to get on with it. If they wanted to kill themselves, I couldn't care less.'

She was laughing all the time she told the crack. Anyway, apparently this had gone on for hours, Dad insisting on taking Eddy back and Eddy insisting on taking Dad back in turn until the car finally ran out of petrol on Jacktrees Road and they left it and walked, and made their way back, Eddy to Cleator and Dad to Cleator Moor on foot.

Mind you, Dad got this final warning last Saturday night for taking the car up the Moor when he was going for a drink. Mam said she would throw the key away if she ever caught him out on a Saturday night with the car again, because he'd gone through the back of the garage in the car. Fortunately it was only made of asbestos, so neither the car or Dad had come to any real harm. The garage needed a new back in it, but that was easily fixed.

What he decided was in future he'd take the car to the Moor and walk back, so Mam reluctantly agreed to this. The problem was on Sunday morning Dad woke me up early and said, 'Sean, get dressed and go round on your bike and find where I've left the car. It could be at Cromwell's or on Earl Street, I can't remember. Don't say a word to your mother, and look sharp because we need the car for ten o'clock Mass. Now remember, say nowt to your mother.'

I did this and found the car outside the Derby Arms. When I got back home I told Dad and he sneaked out to fetch it back while Mam made the breakfast. She was none the wiser, thank God, because she'd have given a right dogging if she ever found out.

I make my Dad out to be a bit of a drunkard, but he wasn't really. He worked most weekends and only went for a pint when he wasn't working on a Sunday, so his drinking antics were a good laugh because he came home full of the joys of spring, usually persuading Mam to put the frying pan on and make him a bacon sandwich. She'd say, 'I don't know why I'm humouring you, Jay, do you think I've got nothing better to do than feed you up after a belly full of beer?'

And he'd say, 'Oh, go on, now, lass, I could eat a scabby horse,' then wink at us as he said, 'Then maybe I'll give you a wee kiss and a cuddle.' She'd soon shift off the settee when he said that, disappearing into the kitchen muttering, 'A kiss and a cuddle, my arse,' and chuckling away fifty to the dozen. Dad would have a grin on his face from ear to ear as he gently eased one buttock off the settee to let off the biggest raspberry you ever heard, settling back down to wait for his bacon butty.

We were simple folks with simple pleasures most of the time. This was silly bugger time for Dad. He had a couple of wee songs, only two to my certain knowledge, and very little voice to go with them, but they went like this – only on a Saturday night, mind:

Wherever I go I take my po and a good supply of paper
And when I'm done I wipe my bum and stick it up a ventilator.

The second one:

Charlie, Charlie, Chuck, Chuck, Chuck
Went to bed with two young ducks
One died, Charlie cried, sitting by the fireside.

We all joined in with his wee bit of fun. Mam would shuffle back with his bacon butty and brown sauce and say, 'Now, get that down ye and go to yer bed before I black your two eyes.' Dad would fidget himself straight and laugh his teeth out, saying, 'Oh, that's just the ticket, Eileen. I don't know what I did to deserve you, lass.'

Mam would answer, 'You're a bloody auld flarch, Jay Close, now git yerself away to bed, do you hear me?'

CHAPTER 12
YURI GAGARIN

We'd suffered a terrible tragedy about that time. We'd always wanted a dog but Mam wouldn't let us have one. We'd had cats and pet mice and just before we left Cleator Mam had come home from Whitehaven market one Thursday with a tortoise for me. Not for anyone else, just for me, because I'd pestered her relentlessly for six months saying, 'All I've ever wanted in my life, my whole life, was a tortoise'. She'd been on the look-out for one ever since.

Finally the day came, out of the blue. I got home from school to find a small cardboard box standing on the draining board. I noticed it straight away and thought it was a box of day-old chickens. Mam often arrived back from the market with day-old chickens for Dad's hen hut, so I went over to it to take a look. Mam stayed silent. I opened the folded lid and couldn't believe my eyes when I saw what was in it.

I shouted to Mam, 'Where did this come from, Mam?'

And she said, 'It's from Whitehaven, and it's yours'. I was too delighted for words.

I picked it out of the box saying, 'Oh, thanks, Mam. It's great! It's just what I've always wanted.'

And she came up to me and put her arms round me and said, 'Now, the man in the pet shop said you have to be very gentle with him, and not throw him around or he'll die. Now, I've got some lettuce to feed him on and he only needs water, not milk, to drink. What do you think?'

I said, 'It's just lovely, Mam. Thank you.'

Well, it's all very well getting a tortoise, but it needs a special name. Not like a cat or a dog. So, after much deliberation I decided on the name Yuri, after the Russian astronaut, Yuri Gagarin. Now, that's a special name, don't you think? Yuri spent many a happy hour staggering, with his big thick shell and wee short legs, from his new wooden tomato box with its cardboard bottom, across the strip of grass on the front garden at Prospect to its lettuce leaf and back again.

At first he would disappear into his shell as soon as I got to within a couple of feet of him, but after a few days he would stretch his gnarled, scaly neck and shove his head high into the air and let me tickle the soft flesh under his chin. I thought he was the best pet anyone could have and all of Cleator came to visit him, to stand back in terror as he approached them without any fear. I fed him and exercised him all summer with great delight, them one afternoon in late September he wouldn't come out of his box and he was scratching his cardboard into shreds into the corner.

When I told Dad he said, 'He must be getting ready for his hibernation.' Which indeed he was, and after about a week of nest-building, with a little help from an old woollen balaclava of mine, he went to sleep for nearly six months. I tucked his box in the cupboard under the stairs and checked on him every single day throughout that winter and spring.

He surfaced for the first time on Easter Sunday Morning. I had noticed for a few days he seemed to have moved position in his nest, but no sign of him sticking his head out for a look. His eyes had been open for at least four days before he finally made his move. We got back from Mass and I went straight to him, and there he was, out of the nest and straining his neck to see where I was. I picked him up and put him straight down to a piece of tender cabbage, which he ate very slowly and managed a wee drink of water. Mam said, 'Put him back into his box and don't bother him until tomorrow.'

After that Yuri was back from his space travel, and up to his old tricks, getting stuck on the rockery stones in the front garden. Mam said I should rename him Jesus, because he rose from the dead on Easter Sunday. I decided, don't ask me why, to paint a dickie-bow on Yuri's shell. The pattern of his shell just at the back of his neck was the perfect shape of a bow-tie, and so I did it with some yellow gloss paint from the lean-to in the back yard. He looked a picture, prancing round the garden in his new bow-tie. If only I had left it at that.

Again, for reasons best known to myself, I decided to complete the job and paint the rest of his shell dark blue. I got the dark blue gloss paint from the lean-to and finished the job. I thought I'd keep the new paint job a secret until the paint had dried and I put him in his little box and shut the lid. The next morning when I went to fetch him out he was dead. His legs were spread out and his head sticking out from the shell resting on the floor. I was beside myself. I realised almost at once that I'd killed him with the paint. I thought the paint fumes had killed him, but Dad said he would suffocate because his shell needed to breathe and the paint would have stopped the shell breathing.

We buried him in the front garden under the rockery and I cried for days. Mam said what I'd done was cruel, but she knew I hadn't done it on purpose, and tried to console me.

CHAPTER 13
SHOT DEAD

Anyhow, that was years ago. I'm well over that now. The tragedy I'm talking about is Kim, the wee black mongrel. Actually, he had a tragic look about him from day one. He started life with us at Seaview Place as a six-week old puppy, newly weaned from his mother. A scruffy, shaggy brown and white thing of unknown lineage and dodgy morals, who had produced a litter of pups regularly every six months or so.

How Mam was persuaded to let him share our house I don't honestly know, because she used to say, 'I don't like dogs. I wouldn't be cruel to them, but I don't like them and I'll never have one in the house.' These were words she'd chew up and spit out, because it arrived. It looked a bit like a tadpole, all fat and shiny black. It soon proved to be the most unfortunate looking dog you could imagine. It had inherited all the worst physical attributes of its millions of predecessors; long skinny legs on a short rickety-looking body, and the worst, scruffiest, mangiest-looking black coat you saw on any dog. It was more like a hyena than a dog, but, oh, how we loved him.

He was coming up to a year old and he had a determination on him to beat the band. Stephen and me took him to puppy training classes at Ehenside school. The woman who took the classes was like Attila the Hun and she could have trained lions, I'm sure, but not Kim. He wouldn't do a bloody thing she told him. He was a disgrace, he really was.

She trailed him round the school hall telling him to 'Heel!'. He just ignored her. 'Sit!' was a foreign language to him. He'd just look at her as she pushed his bum to the floor, repeating, 'Sit! Sit!'. Just a waste of time. He'd look at her as he rose from the floor and just silently say, 'No. Why should I? Not for you, anyhow.'

All the other pups were jumping through hoops after a month with Attila, but not Kim. She couldn't master him. After an intensive course of nightly training from Stephen and me he succumbed to 'Sit!' now and again, but 'Stay!' never. And he wouldn't give her the satisfaction of any manoeuvres whatsoever at the classes, so eventually to Kim's and Attila's relief we stopped the classes and got as much obedience from him as we could without beating him with a stick, which is what Dad said he needed.

One day Stephen, my cousin Raymond Graham and my next-door neighbour Malcolm Tate and myself were playing on the big hill when we heard the shot ring out. It sounded quite near, and we all remarked on hearing it, then continued our commando raid on the big hill cave. When we got home for our tea I noticed a trail of blood leading from the end of the path to the back door, and I ran in shouting, 'Mam! There's blood on the path!' Mam was standing in the kitchen crying, and poor wee Kim was propping himself up against the wall on all fours in a small pool of blood. Mam said, 'I think he's been shot, Sean, because he's covered in holes.' The poor wee bugger! Who would do a trick like that?

Kim was one for the hens – he loved to chase them. Every time we took him anywhere near a farmyard we had to put him on his lead because he'd be off like a shot after hens and ducks, coming back with a mouthful of feathers, often as not. So we were careful not to let him near them.

His last day on this earth had started off a happy one, because he'd had his walk down the church road and back again, and somehow, after we'd left for the big hill, he'd got out in the garden and found a hole in the hawthorn hedge separating the car park from Abe Woodburn's field. True to form, he'd made his way to Abe's farmyard, which was a stone's throw from our house, and got in among the hens, or so Abe said when Dad went round to find out why he'd shot him.

Mam had heard the gunshots just the other side of our fence in the field and ran out to see what was going on. She couldn't see any sign of anybody, and thought it must be kids with an air rifle, then discovered Kim was missing. She assumed we'd taken him with us and thought no more about it until half an hour or so later she heard him crying at the back door. She opened the door and he slumped over the threshold onto the outhouse floor.

Dad arrived in from work at half past four. He picked some of the pellets out of him with a pair of tweezers and bathed the wound with Dettol and warm water. When we arrived Dad had just gone over to Abe's, like a madman, Mam said, and he hadn't got back. When he finally got back he came into the house, ashen-faced and said, 'That old bugger won't be shooting any more dogs for a long time, I can tell you.'

Mam said, 'My God, Jay, what have you done to him?'

And he said, 'I've nearly wrapped the bloody rifle round his neck. He shot that dog at point blank range, Eileen. It didn't stand a chance.'

Mam said, 'Have you hurt Abe?'

And Dad said, 'Too true, I've hurt him. I'm going to the police station to report it right now. Abe's not badly hurt, but I've taught him a lesson and I'd better let the police know before they come looking for me.'

Abe didn't press charges against Dad, and Dad took four chickens round to him to replace the ones he claimed Kim had worried, and poor old Kim died standing up against the kitchen wall. He had so many pellets in him, he couldn't bear the pain of lying down.

There was much wailing and gnashing of teeth in our house that night, and no consoling any of us, including Mam, who wouldn't have a dog in the house, by her talk.

The next day Dad took Stephen and me and the Tate's lads and my cousin Raymond from next door to Drigg beach, where he said we could look for grass snakes in the sand dunes. We found half a dozen of the things and Dad tried to cheer us up, letting the snakes crawl round his neck and down his shirt, but there was no lifting my spirits that day. All I could think about was Kim and the cruel way he met his end, and how I was going to miss the scruffy wee mite.

Nana Heron said, 'Eileen, you should get another dog straight away for them wee kids, they're heart-broken.' So within the week Flicka arrived. Now, she was another kettle of fish altogether. She was a cocker-spaniel cross. Her father was a boxer. Hard to imagine it, isn't it? She was ninety percent cocker to look at, but had a broader face and shorter legs than the full breed, but she had the ears. Oh!, she had the ears. Long, black, thick curly ears. Poor old Kim didn't have ears, well, none to speak of. His were more like tears in his head, but Flicka had proper ears. You could spend hours brushing and combing them, and she let you. She loved getting them ears played with. She was eleven months old when we got her, fully house-trained, never did so much as a pump in the house, Mam told Nana.

Nana was delighted for us. She said, 'That wee dog will be the makings of them kids, our Eileen, after what they've just been through. And so it was, Flicka would soon repair all the broken hearts and add so much pleasure and joy to our lives.

CHAPTER 14
NANA HERON'S HAIRNET

Talking of Nana Heron, she'd given them all a bit of a fright. Papa had been down to our house to build a coal bunker for Mam and one for Aunty Lily at the back of the houses. Mam says since he's retired he's dying to make himself useful and they don't want the coals kept in the house on account of the dust. So Papa, to our delight, had been in residence for four days constant.

He always wore a dark grey suit with a waistcoat and a big gold pocket watch and chain. He always wore a tie and his black leather boots used to shine like a shitten stick. This was his retirement uniform – he was a very smart old man. Resplendent in his weekday suit he meticulously built the coalhouses from wooden boards and corrugated tin, and when they were finished they would have withstood an earthquake.

Mam and Aunty Lily were demented with him, trailing all the muck of the day through their houses as he trundled in and out with his boots full of gutters, but they would never have complained to him for they idolised him and wouldn't offend him for their lives. On his last day of building the bunkers he happened to remark that May-Lizzie (Nana) wasn't so good when he left her in the morning, and she'd complained of a buzzing in her head that had got on her nerves.

Mam was a bit worried about her and went back with Papa to see her when he'd finished his work. She'd spent the day nursing what she called a nuisance rather than a pain. Apparently the buzzing came and went at irregular intervals and seemed to be easing off. Aunty May had told Mam she'd wanted to send for the doctor but Mammy wouldn't hear tell of it, but if it hadn't stopped by the morning she was sending for him, whether Mammy wants him or not. Nana had spent the day sitting in her rocking chair, which was one of a set of two chairs, the rocker for her and a matching upholstered standard armchair for Papa.

The living room on Kier Hardy Avenue was a large square room which led on from the front hall. It had a wooden picture rail with three beautiful prints of some Scottish landscape with Highland cattle and mountains and lakes, all framed in matching heavy gilt frames. The wallpaper up to the picture rail was a leafy pattern, with subtle light brown and green swathes of colour. There was a walnut writing bureau and a walnut china cabinet with the loveliest china dinner service, tea sets, crystal glasses and cake stands.

Nana had good taste. She liked good quality furniture, and the room being large, housed a beautiful black-as-black piano, defying you to find a scratch on it. Everything was shining to perfection (Aunty May's department). Papa had taken the old range out and replaced it with a more modern tile grate. The room smelt of polish and pipe tobacco and I thought it was the loveliest room in the world. All the daughters had been married from 26 Kier Hardy Avenue, and the house had a timeless quality about it to me. It felt as if it had been there for ever.

Mam left feeling slightly reassured and told Aunty May to let her know in the morning how Nana was. Well, she needn't have worried, because the next morning Aunty May made her usual early morning visit to Aunty Lily's and summoned Mam for a detailed update. May and Lily were in tucks when Mam went over the back garden to Aunty Lily's, and when May finally stopped laughing she told Mam, 'Eileen, I'm sorry, lass, that you've been worried about Mammy, but she's champion now, the buzzing stopped just before she went to bed about 10 o'clock. She hadn't had a buzz for over an hour and she started to get herself ready for bed. When she took her hairnet off, she shouted from the bathroom for me to come and see what she'd found, and there in the hairnet was a dead wasp.'

Mam started to laugh and said, 'Well, I'll go to hell. Is that what the buzzing had been?' And May and Lily were hysterical, May going over every buzz and telling them how she'd made her sit quiet all day and brought her beef tea and a boiled egg for her dinner, for fear of making her sick with anything heavier. Mam said, 'We're laughing now, but I've been worried sick. I thought she had a brain tumour.' And Aunty Lily saying, 'Thank God we didn't get the doctor out!'

Mam said, 'What did Daddy have to say?' and Aunty May said, 'Oh, he's not amused. When I started to tell Alice next door this morning he shouted me in and said, 'Now, you can cut that out and stop telling everybody, May. You're not making a cuddy out of her. Now, do you hear me?' Lily said, 'God love him, Eileen, he wouldn't let anybody take a rise out of Mammy, or any of us for that matter'. The giggles continued.

CHAPTER 15
THE ANNUAL TRIP
TO BOWNESS KNOTT

I would say that my Dad could be best described as being of a creative nature. He always had some project or scheme of some sort or another on the go. He makes holly wreaths which he sells for extra Christmas money, a skill he acquired in his apprenticeship days at the market gardens at Cleator and which he involves us lads in.

Every year around late November we would be trundled into his old blue Bedford van and deposited at a convenient lay-by on the fell road, handy for the swathes of bracken which skirted the lower fell sides of Dent. The bracken would have gone a deep russet colour by then and be tinder dry. Dad would provide us with a plenteous supply of Hessian sacks and some stout leather gauntlets to protect our hands and lower arms from the sharp cut stems of the bracken. Dad used some strange-looking secateurs which looked like they belonged to a torture chamber to cut the bracken and our job was to collect it. We were kept well away from the secateurs because of their lethal possibilities. Mam wouldn't have appreciated one of us coming home minus a limb. After the sacks had been filled and loaded into the van we would all pile into the back on top of the soft, plump bags of harvested bracken. We would be bounced from one end of the van to the other all the way home, loving every minute of it.

That wasn't quite the end of our involvement. Dad would lay the bracken over a series of frames he'd made and placed in the roof section of the garden shed for the final couple of weeks, drying before they were made into the wreath bases. Dad had inherited a cuddy-load of rusty wire wreath bases, circular in shape, from an old man who had finished wreath-making, so the profit margin in the wreaths would be higher this year (not having to buy in the wire bases). Between now and the second week of December Dad would spend every minute of his spare time moulding the dry bracken leaves to the wire bases, forming a plump, round sausage shape using fine tie wire to secure the wadding and trimming off the excess with strong scissors.

When this was completed (which seemed to take forever), they would be stacked one on top of another and hung in bunches of twelve on hooks on the hut wall ready for the next stage. I was always in his face during these mad weeks leading up to Christmas, because I wanted to learn how to make the wreaths, so in spite of his busy schedule, he'd teach me his wreath-making skills.

My first attempt at forming a wreath ring looked more like a badly plastered broken arm, all lumps and bumps and uneven surfaces, but after watching Dad and learning by my mistakes, I soon produced a half-decent plump round sausage shape and was promptly put on the production line. Dad told me I was a natural at it, and like him I was born to work. (He's been right about that.)

The next stage was in fact my favourite, because once again it involved us lads and any of our mates we cared to take along. In the van again, and this time we head for Gillerthwaite to look for berry holly. Now, this berry holly is a bit of an elusive commodity. You can't rely on it turning up on the same tree every year, so you have to go out and find it. Dad had an arrangement with the farmers from Gillerthwaite; don't ask me what it was – probably one of his hound-trailing deals. No money ever changed hands, it was a favour for a favour, maybe a couple of wreaths for an afternoon in berry holly valley.

Well, as it happened this particular year, berry holly valley, it wasn't. We parked the van half a mile past Bowness Knott in a gateway leading to an old rope suspension bridge across the bottom of the Lisa just where it enters the top of Ennerdale Lake. This bridge was suspended awkwardly either side of the river between trees, and the ropes had rough planks of wood across them to form a footbridge, rickety to say the least. When you got to the middle of the bridge you could swing the whole thing in every direction, including up and down.

This of course we did, Dad being oblivious of the fact that he was practically walking at an angle of forty-five degrees and swinging like the rib-tickler at Cleator Moor fair. He was totally focused on the hunt and keeping his eyes peeled for the elusive red berry. The whole day was an adventure because the Lisa meanders down the valley from the top of Black Sail and Windy Gap through Lowther Forest and down to enter the lake.

We spent the afternoon crossing the river in the shallows and re-crossing across the rapids, so we weren't really bothered if we never saw a single holly berry. The fewer we saw the further the walk would be. The plan was to collect as much berry holly as we could carry between us and leave the berry-less holly till the last thing, when we were almost back at the van, because the valley was alive with barren holly trees. We knew from past years not to strip a tree of berries, just take a small amount from each tree, leaving the bulk of it for the birds, was our instruction from Dad. You haven't to be greedy with Mother Nature, he used to say.

The bottom of Gillerthwaite Valley stands at the top of Ennerdale Lake and it's only three or four miles from Cleator Moor, but what a different world it presents! The minute you get out of the van you can sense the wildness of the place; the smell of pine in the wind, the eerie silence, broken only by the occasional cry of the golden eagle as it spirals upwards above the fells on the passing thermals. Dad showed us badgers' setts, foxholes and the remains of more birds' nests than I can name, including buzzards, high up in the rocky crags.

We loved these Gillerthwaite treks. We often saw young deer drinking at the beck edge, nervously taking a sip and looking all around, sensing our presence and swiftly making off into the woods to safety. It was a bit like an Outward Bound course, with Dad the leader, driving us on through streams and bog lands, disregarding our less than adequate foot wear. Within half an hour our best attempts at keeping our feet dry would be thwarted by Dad's instructions. ('Never mind your feet, keep your eyes open for berry holly.')

Mam used to go mad at the state he brought us back in, but he didn't care. He'd just say, 'For crying out loud, Eileen, would you give it a rest? We've been up the fells, lass, not on a bloody picnic!'

To which Mam would chunter some response on the lines of, 'Aye, well, it's all very well for you, Jay, you don't have to get their shoes dry.'

A truce would soon be reached between them, usually with Dad taking our shoes into the kitchen sink, scrubbing them and stuffing them with newspapers, placing them round the living room fire to dry. Mam would have a face like bad fat for the rest of the night, because she'd have to sit looking at them, decorating her hitherto tidy hearth.

We never ever took a scrap of food with us on any of Dad's treks – not even an apple, so needless to say we'd be lepping with the hunger by the time we got back home some four or five hours later and ready to eat Mam out of house and home.

The next stage of the wreath-making was filling the wreaths with holly. This was done by clipping three to four inch pieces of holly from the branches, stripping the last few leaves off and twisting a piece of nine-inch straight wire round the end of the twig of holly. This done, the more skilful job of threading the straight wires through the wreath base had to be done. The secret was to stab the wreath base with the wire very quickly and go straight through in one go, otherwise you'd bend the wire and have to start again with a new piece of wire. This could be costly, as the bent wires couldn't be re-used.

Once the whole base is covered with holly, so that none of the base is visible, the precious berry holly twigs can be strategically put into place, usually six bunches per wreath. Dad usually made between thirty and forty wreaths in one go and if any more were required he'd make them to order. He sold some to a couple of greengrocer's shops on the Moor, but the majority went to relatives and neighbours, he was never left with any on his hands, in fact, I don't think he ever had enough for the demand, but he was limited by the spare time he had.

The last time Dad made holly wreaths was December, 1962, the worst berry holly season in living memory. There just wasn't any berries on any of the trees. After three or four fruitless trips to Gillerthwaite that year he abandoned the idea of berries and went for making his own waxed paper lilies to furnish the wreaths and made only a handful or so. I think it sickened him for ever and meant we'd lost our annual trek up the fells with him. A sad year for all of us.

The reason I started to tell you about the holly wreaths in the first place is because I'm standing in the garden shed looking up at the roof, being reminded of the wreaths by one solitary wire wreath ring, the only surviving one. I can also see the remnants of a canoe in the roof timbers. It does look a bit odd if you don't know how the canoe timber got there, but I know, because I was with Dad when he made the hut, and he told me how he came by these curved pieces of timber, all polished and smooth against the rest of the wood, which was as rough as a badger's arse.

CHAPTER 16
JAY'S FLYING MACHINE

When we lived at Cleator, Dad had a particular period of creativity. He made a sledge out of some roof timbers (second-hand). This sledge was more like a Trojan warrior's battering ram than your usual poncy sleigh. It was about five feet long, so that we could all get on it at once 'so there'd be no-one fighting' (as if!) he said. It consisted of two nine-inch by two-inch roof joists for runners held together by two-foot wide four-inch by two-inch floor joists. It weighed about as much as a small settee. I know, because I helped carry it from Prospect to the Glebe field at Cleator for its maiden voyage.

When the snow finally arrived we'd been looking at it in the back yard for weeks praying for snow to try it out. When the first snows came that winter we carried it with great effort between Barry, Stephen and myself, because it was too heavy to pull along in the snow. (We should have known then.) When we finally arrived at the top of the slope, exhausted from our efforts, we placed the sledge on the shiny surface of the already flattened snow and watched it sink like the Titanic.

Barry tried to pull it out of its pit to a firmer position, but it stuck fast. When we eventually re-floated it and brought it further down the slope Barry gave it a push and to our delight it started to move. He shouted instructions to Stephen and me to jump on while it was moving, which we did. We all landed on it at once and it went down like a lead sinker into the snow. I mean, not down the slope. We were made a proper laughing stock by it with the older lads. They christened the sledge Jay's Flying Machine and we dragged the numb thing to the Lonnie bridge and launched it over the handrail, never to be seen again.

Dad wasn't exactly chuffed when we told him about it, but agreed he had thought it had been a bit weighty. That was one of Dad's mega understatements, for which he was famous.

CHAPTER 17
THE CANOE IN THE ATTIC

Undeterred by the failure of Jay's Flying Machine, Dad embarked on a much more ambitious project to while away the winter nights. This project was his first attempt at boat-building. Well, actually, to be precise, canoe building. He'd acquired a proper set of plans, including written instructions, and a sketch of how the canoe would look when completed. A step-by-step building guide, in fact.

He set the whole thing up in the attic on a set of trestles and worked on it religiously after work for months. We slept in the attic and spent many an hour playing in the half-constructed hull after we were sent to bed and by late February of that year the canoe was nearly finished. Dad had bought some canvas to cover the frame and he was going to cover the canvas with fibre glass once he had secured it to the frame.

It was at this point that Mam, on one of her visits to watch the master at work, just happened to remark that she hoped it would go down the attic stairs alright. Dad nearly jumped down her neck. 'Of course it'll go down the stairs, woman! Do you think I'm an eejit or something? That's just typical of you, Eileen, you have to look on the black side of things every time,' he said. 'You know how to take the arse out of things alright.'

'Oh, I'm very sorry,' said Mam rather sarcastically. 'I just think it looks a bit big for that bottom turn, that's all. But I'll keep my remarks to myself in future.' She flounced off down the stairs with the wind out of her sails.

Dad chuntered away for a while and kept standing back from the canoe and looked like he was weighing things up. Eventually he took his tape measure and went to the bottom of the stairs. He began to take measurements of the door opening and then the distances between the door and the top of the cat winder; then diagonal measurements. He was bouncing from the stairs to the canoe measuring, then from the canoe back to the stairs. This bout of frantic measuring continued for a quarter of an hour or so, and finally resulted in Dad standing over the canoe frame scratching his head and saying, 'I don't believe it. I bloody-well don't believe it.'

We knew better than to make too many comments at this juncture and kept agreeing with him when we thought that that was what he wanted us to do. He looked at Stephen and me and said, 'Well, I'll go to hell, lads. It looks like your mother was right. The bloody thing won't go down the stairs.' He shouted Mam to come up and she clambered up the stairs and said, 'My God, man, what's the matter? I thought there'd been an accident or something.' To which Dad replied, 'You could say that, lass. You were right.,' he said. 'I'm going to have to take the whole thing to bits to get it down the stairs.'

Mam said, 'Oh, Jay, lad. After all the work you've put in, what a damn shame.' 'Aye, well,' said Dad. 'I didn't think for a minute it wouldn't go down the stairs, but I hadn't taken into account that turn at the bottom. I hadn't even thought about it till you mentioned it,' he said. 'Sorry I shouted at you, lass. You know how it is.' Mam put her arm round his neck and said, 'What a crying shame, lad. I feel that sorry for you. It's just real bad luck.'

After a few attempts at physically trying to get it down the stairs, Stephen and me at one end and Dad at the other and getting stuck like Winnie the Pooh every time, Dad abandoned the idea and we gave up for the night.

The canoe laid on the trestles in the attic looking like the skeleton of Brontosaurus Rex for weeks, until finally, after a load of pestering from Mam about cluttering up the attic, Dad dismantled the canoe, placed the numbered parts into several Hessian bags and stacked them against the far wall, where they remained until we moved to Cleator Moor some years later. But, as I said before, some of the canoe frame has ended up in the hut roof, where it shall remain as a constant reminder of Dad's folly in the attic that winter. I don't know how we can bear to look at it.

CHAPTER 18
NELLIE BENNETT
BACK AT SAINT CUTHBERT'S

One of our younger teachers was Miss Bennett, Nellie. She was our Poetry Appreciation tutor and she introduced me to a world of beautiful words. She taught me to ponder over and to wallow in some of the most fantastic poetry and prose ever written. Her love of poetry rubbed off on me and I was able to be transported in thought to the mystic world of Abu Ben Adam, the high seas of the Ancient Mariner and the American prairies of Hiawatha, to name but a few.

Her lessons were a period of escapism for my fertile mind. I must have been emotionally starved before Nellie Bennett came into my life. Part of the attraction of poetry appreciation was listening to Nellie reading the poetry to us. She used such expression in her voice. She painted a picture in our minds. I was mesmerised by her, but most importantly she introduced me to a life-long appreciation and love of poetry.

In our family we didn't wear our feelings on our sleeves. We weren't the sort of family who told each other we loved them. We didn't exchange many hugs and kisses and we weren't good at expressing our feelings. We all looked out for each other and loved each other deeply but weren't taught to express our feelings. Being kind to each other and respectful of each other and to share what we had with each other was the way we were taught to love, so to listen to and to read poetry opened up a whole new world of expression to me. It changed the way I was able to relate to other people. In some ways it gave me the confidence to express myself in what could have been interpreted as a rather precocious way, which on odd occasions backfired on me.

One such occasion involved Miss Bennett. You see, it's a fine line you tread between a fondness you have for a certain teacher at a tender age, the boundaries of which can become blurred. I felt a certain affinity with Nellie Bennett because of our mutual love of poetry, and I must have overstepped the boundary on this occasion. It was during the rehearsals of the school's production of the Gilbert and Sullivan operetta, The Mikado. St Cuthbert's was famous for its epic productions of Gilbert and Sullivan. The whole school took part in this annual event. Our music, woodwork and art lessons were dominated by making scenery and props for these productions. Cecil B De Mille would have been proud of them.

I was a third-year and had auditioned for a minor part, assistant to Poobah, a role which mainly demanded carrying a canvas canopy to shade the venerable man from the strong sunlight. But to my dismay, I was pipped at the post by my twin brother, Stephen, something I had to muster up all the brotherly love I had to forgive him for. I was relegated to the ranks of the chorus and during rehearsals, which mainly took place after school hours during the winter months, my presence was only required on stage for a short period of time.

Miss Bennett was often in attendance behind the scenes, keeping order and prompting the principals. I was standing next to her backstage and was engaged in conversation with her, and the conversation was of a more relaxed nature than that of the classroom due to the circumstances and we were talking on a very personal level, one which I was comfortable with, but out of the blue Miss Bennett stopped me short and told me not to be so cheeky and disrespectful. I hadn't realised I'd overstepped the boundary of teacher/pupil propriety and had deeply offended her.

She was furious with me to such an extent that she pushed me (harder than she thought, I suspect) and I found myself falling backwards down the backstage steps and landing on my backside, more shocked than hurt. I can't even remember what it was I said to offend her. I think I had a bit of a crush on her and, discovering this, she found it necessary to nip it in the bud. This was to be a salutary lesson for me and in future I was more careful not to be too familiar with any of my teachers.

The Mikado was a colourful and exotic experience for me and a huge success, bringing packed houses every night for a full week. Cleator Moor had more than its fair share of talented singers – the Irish influence, I suspect. My new-found confidence had been slighted dented by my run-in with Miss Bennett, but my love of Gilbert and Sullivan had been firmly rooted. The roar of the crowd and the smell of the greasepaint brought its own rewards.

CHAPTER 19
A TEENAGER IN THE 1960S

Being a teenager in the 1960s was quite different from being a teenager in any previous era, because, for a start, the word 'teenager' had just been invented. Teenagers prior to 1960 had no status. They were previously regarded as adolescents making the transition between childhood and adulthood. They were not expected to have any opinion. They were on a learning curve, and as such, were considered by adults to be inconsequential. Not so for the 1960s teenagers. We were catapulted into the public arena by television. Teenagers were being interviewed by journalists and put under the microscope publicly for the first time, mainly because of the pop music circus which was rapidly gaining momentum.

Love Me Do

'Love Me Do' was the first ever Beatles' hit. I remember the first time I heard it on the radio; it hit me like an explosion. It was the most exciting sound I'd ever heard. It's hard to explain how a musical sound can have such a huge effect on a young ear, but the sound shocked and excited me at the same time. You can actually hear you own heart beating and you want to hear it over and over again. In fact we played 'Love Me Do' on our radiogram so many times on Sunday afternoons that Mam said if we didn't play something else she was going to smash it into smithereens.

The only other pop song to evoke similar emotions in me prior to the Beatles was 'Wimoweh', but it paled into insignificance against the bang-up-to-date Mersey sound. It was just the most incredible, evocative and sexually arousing sound ever to be produced by man. Listening to it was like an orgasm in sound; it could lift you to a higher level.

When the Beatles were played at the record hops, the dance floor would be choc-a-bloc. Not a single person was left sitting or standing round the edges. Even if you didn't have a partner you could just join another couple or just stand on your own and shuffle around. You couldn't do nothing – it was impossible.

Actually, 'Love Me Do' was a Jive tune, unlike many others of the Beatles later hits, but the Twist was at its height at the record hops, so some people did the Twist to it, others did the Jive. I favoured the Jive, because of the physical contact with your partner, and because the man was in control of the dance steps. He dictated the moves and could surprise his partner and woo her with his display of complicated dance steps, spinning her around and pulling her in to him at will. It was a power dance and the man reigned supreme.

With the decline of the Jive in the early 1960s came the death of male dominance on the dance floor. Sexual equality kicked in – kicked us lads in the balls, without a doubt. The cut and chase was removed from the dance floor and the very dull, sterile, unskilful excuse for a dance took its place. No physical contact between partners, no holding hands, no returning the girl back to her seat, no thank you for the dance. The rules for pre-sexual interaction were suddenly drastically changed for ever.

The Twist had started the trend of partners doing their own thing, but the Shift completed the move. Instead of complicated, skilful dance steps which took a lot of concentration and energy, you had the very boring, practically static non-movement of the new dance, not to mention never getting within two feet of the very sexy, skinny-ribbed mini-skirt-clad beauties allegedly dancing with you.

The dance was no longer a sharing of movement in unison, a graceful brush of breasts against the chest, the erotic hint of the subtle perfume effusing from a milky-white neck or a slim wrist as you twined between each other to the tune of 'Rock Around the Clock'. It had become a lone pleasure, a way of experiencing your individual interpretation of the music. No need of a partner, no flash of a firm cleavage, no exchanging of body odours, no bodily contact, in fact no physical interaction of any sort. It was self-gratification on a grand scale. Public masturbation (well, not quite). Life would never be the same again.

CHAPTER 20
JOHNNIE MORRIS

Johnnie Morris. He was our science teacher. A larger than life bombastic, sort of fellow. The common man's Jimmy Edwards. He had no problem with discipline, in fact he doled out his punishment in a rather unique way. He used a Bunsen burner tube. Three lashes of a two-feet-long Bunsen burner tube wrapped around your hand taught you not to mess with Johnnie Morris, and no mistake.

He was sound, though. A good, dedicated teacher who genuinely liked kids. There were a couple of lads who were special needs cases, and there was nothing in place at our school for such lads; they would slip though the net if individual teachers didn't take them under their wings. Johnnie was one such teacher. He had these lads working in the school greenhouses and tending the cold frames, giving them a sense of purpose and keeping them out of trouble.

He was a strange mixture of academic and pig farmer mentality. His general appearance was untidy and unkempt. His lessons were a great source of pleasure and amusement to me. He had the ability to make a really dull lesson on the single-cell amoeba stick in your mind forever, suggesting there were at least six lads in our class with the same amount of brain cells on a good day.

I wasn't too keen on biology, but I loved botany, the study of plants. He taught me all about taking plant cuttings from stems and leaves, and introduced me to a life-long interest in growing things from seed, propagating plants from plants – again a good example of teacher's enthusiasm rubbing off on his pupils.

He was a bit of a trapper. He spent much of his leisure time in outdoor pursuits such as rabbiting and fishing. He could often be seen with his terriers and a group of these less able lads setting off on hunting expeditions at weekends. You had to be physically up to Johnnie's jaunts, because he did everything at breakneck speed, so he had no time for wimps.

It Seemed a Good Idea at the Time

I'd never actually been on any of his Saturday morning treks, but when he announced he was planning a week's camping expedition to Drigg for third-year lads, Stephen and me put our names down. It was to be in the May half-term holiday. We'd had several weeks to plan our trip and we'd been encouraged by Johnnie to suggest the sort of activities we would like to pursue. Top of the list for most of the lads was rabbiting, which was well-received by the man himself.

I don't really know why I'd been so keen to go on this trip, except to say I found any adventure which took me to new places exciting. I wasn't into hunting any helpless animals at all; I was more into nurture and conservation, and felt sure the trip would include these elements. How is it possible to get things so wrong?

In the weeks running up to the half-term holiday Johnnie had encouraged us to bring supplies into his science lessons; tinned items and non-perishable goods, and before we left for Drigg we had amassed a significant cache of foodstuffs which looked capable of sustaining Hannibal's army for its assault on the high Atlas mountains, never mind our week's jaunt to Drigg. As it turned out, the high Atlas mountains would have been a breeze compared with the sand dunes of Drigg beach.

The due date arrived, and a convoy of three cars and a mini-bus set off from the school gates. We went like lambs to the slaughter. Johnnie was accompanied by another member of staff, Mr Darrigan, and another man I didn't know. Mr Darrigan, Danny as he was known to us, was also the scout master, so his role up to date had been to supply us with the necessary tents and camping equipment. Danny and the other man would be helping supervise during the day time and leaving early evening to return the next day (no bad idea, I'd say) leaving Johnnie in sole charge at night.

We were all full of the joys of Spring on arriving at Drigg beach, after a bit of trouble getting the vehicles on to the sand dunes. We commenced with the arduous task of erecting the bell tent and other smaller tents which would serve as our living and eating quarters for the duration. These tents must have been ex-army, probably left over from World War I by the look of them, with more bits pieced into them than a patch-work quilt. I remember thinking, 'If these tents keep water out, I'll eat my hat'. Mind you, I was wrong about that. They proved to be as water-tight as a duck's arse, which was just as well, because it rained constantly for the whole week.

The bell tent took an age to erect, because the high winds kept lifting it and five or six lads off the ground every time we attempted to raise the centre pole.

Eventually, with the help of the older men and the entire troop, we managed to make it steadfast. The rain in due course eased off, but didn't stop completely. A fine drizzle persisted for the rest of the day and into the evening. We set up tarpaulin awnings for shelters. These would serve as kitchen areas and a place to sit and eat our meals. This is where the nightmare begins. It was decided by Johnnie not to use the food we'd brought with us for our first meal, we'd go hunting instead and see what we came up with.

CHAPTER 21
MYXOMATOSIS
AND RADIATION FEVER

Drigg beach is situated between Seascale and Ravenglass, about three or four miles along the beach from Sellafield. Drigg Dump, as it was known locally, was situated just a few hundred yards inland from the sand dunes where we were camping. The joke circulating round the camp suggested that we needn't worry about lights in the tents at night, because after a couple of days or so, so close to the dump, we'd all be glowing in the dark.

Drigg Dump was where all the contaminated waste from Sellafield Atomic Energy plant was buried and we were camping within earshot of it. (It was beginning, even at this early juncture, to dawn on me that conservation issues would be a low priority for this expedition.) How we'd even managed to get permission to camp on the sand dunes, which were littered with unexploded rifle cartridges (Drigg being a wartime munitions factory and firing range), was a mystery to me. We found dozens of spent and not-so-spent cartridges within a few yards of our camp and were told not to meddle with them, they could go off in our hands. (No second telling was necessary, I can tell you.)

Adders were also a hazard to look out for in the sand dunes, because they were known to be poisonous. Johnnie told us not to worry about grass snakes; they were green and bigger than the adder, but if we spotted a small black snake with a zigzag pattern down its back, that was an adder and to give it a wide berth. When we asked what we should do if we were bitten by an adder he replied, 'Get somebody to suck the poison out and make sure not to swallow it or you could both end up dead.' This was a reassuring piece of information, especially as we were three quarters of an hour from a hospital and not in possession of any antidote. Suddenly survival was the name of the game.

We were all sent out in our small groups of four or five lads equipped with rabbit snares and Hessian bags. Johnnie had previously shown us how to set the snares round the rabbit holes and left us with the sobering news that if we wanted to eat that night, we'd better catch a rabbit. Myxomatosis was rife among the rabbit population of Britain at this time. It had been introduced by the Ministry of Agriculture a couple of years earlier to cull the rabbit population which was out of control and doing untold damage to farmers' crops.

The numbers were drastically down by now and the rabbit population was at a sustainable level. However, Sellafield had reintroduced the disease into the area surrounding the nuclear plant and Drigg Dump because they weren't being naturally culled by poachers and farmers due to the high security around these areas. They were also considered to be at risk of contamination from radiation and could be a risk to the public. More negative points for nurture and conservation.

Our group consisted of Stephen and me, Arty McLaughlin, Bobby Gallagher and Martin Foley. We were lucky enough to catch a rabbit within the first few minutes of our hunt. (I'm not sure 'lucky' is the correct word.) In fact, we didn't so much catch the rabbit as the rabbit gave itself up. It was absolutely wick with Myxi. We'd stumbled upon it by chance. It was crouching behind a clump of gorse half dead. Its face was a mass of broken sores and it had huge lumps growing out of its neck and back, classic symptoms of Myxomatosis. The poor buggers suffered the most appallingly painful and prolonged death imaginable. Surely there must be a more humane way to cull them. Arty McLaughlin said, 'If Johnnie Morris thinks I'm eating anything like this for my supper, he's got another think coming.'

We moved on along the dunes a short way, and saw several of what looked like healthy rabbits running away in the distance, but how could we be sure they were clear of the disease? The consensus of opinion among the group was a ban on eating rabbits. We'd have to use some of the food we'd brought with us for tonight's meal. In spite of the persistent drizzle we patrolled the sand dunes nearly as far as the Ravenglass estuary before we decided to return to camp and inform the bold Johnnie we weren't eating poisonous vermin.

By the time we got back the rest of the group had returned and were busy making the fire from logs we'd brought with us. We had primus stoves, but the boss had decided we'd go for the wild outdoor hunter's method of cooking for as long as the wood lasted. Hopefully we could replenish our stock of fuel with driftwood as the week progressed, he said. We could see four rabbits skinned and strung up round the tent poles, dripping with blood and being licked by one of Johnnie's dogs. This was to be our supper. Our Stephen said to me, 'There'd better be something else to eat, because I'm not touching that lot.'

Johnnie wanted to know why we hadn't caught anything, especially as we'd been away the longest. Martin Foley said, 'Sir, all these rabbits have got Myxi. We've seen one rabbit nearly dead, covered in lumps and scabs, so we're not eating any rabbits. It's not safe to eat, Sir.'

Johnnie said, 'You're talking out of your arse, as usual, Foley. There's no Myxomatosis around here, it's been gone for years.'

We all joined in to support Martin, saying he was wrong. We'd heard Sellafield had reintroduced it, and none of us was prepared to risk it. So Johnnie pulled down one of the skinned rabbits and hung it in front of us and said, 'Look at this rabbit. It's as healthy a rabbit as I've seen in years. It's got no disease of any kind and you're all having it for your suppers.'

'Well, I'll go hungry rather than eat that', I said, 'I don't care what he says. Besides, the bloody dog's been licking it after licking its own arse. I've got two packets of chocolate digestive biscuits in my rucksack, that will do for Stephen and me for tonight.'

A feeling of unease was developing in the camp. Johnnie had got us all peeling potatoes and several large tins of peas had been placed next to the camp fire. He'd erected a tripod of steel bars above the fire and one of the rabbits was hanging like a dead babby from it. The smoke and flames were lapping round it and juices from it were dripping and being spat back by the flames. I decided I'd take the meat and hide it in my pocket till later. I'd eat the peas and potatoes, but definitely not the rabbit.

This atmosphere set the tone for the remainder of our trip. The weather worsened the following morning after a night of high winds and gentle rain. The tent hadn't let us down and the crack had been great. We'd lain awake for hours in the bell tent, all twelve of us, toe to toe in a circle, exchanging the filthiest jokes and tales about lasses we'd been with, all made up of course.

Sleep had finally come to all of us, and so did the morning. It was Sunday morning, and you couldn't see three feet in front of you.

The rain was intermittent, so we had our cornflakes and boiled eggs in silence, secretly cursing the weather under the tarpaulin.

Our first planned event of the day after we washed up was a trek along the beach to Seascale for eleven o'clock Mass. The weather showed no signs of improvement as we trundled along the sand, and we were going to have to rely on the Sunday service to rekindle our will to live, because most of us had lost it by now.

CHAPTER 22
THE MASS FROM HELL

The Mass was being held in a big old house at the end of a row of guest houses and large private houses on the top of a hill overlooking the sea front. I think the priest lived in the house and used the very large living room for Sunday Mass. No catholic church had been built in Seascale and because of the contractors building Sellafield, many of whom were Irish, a need for a temporary parish had developed.

Our numbers were about to overload the system and cause a bit of friction, because it wasn't really possible to get everybody in, never mind seated. Eventually, after Johnnie pushed his way in and wedged us into any available space round the room, we all settled down in a standing position to hear the holy Mass. The priest came in through the only door in the rear of the room, and had to practically walk across a sea of heads in order to gain access to the altar. He made a joke about the parting of the waves by Moses, and raised a few muffled titters.

Well, to say the experience was not very uplifting, standing soaked to the pelt for a full hour among a group of smelly Irish navvies, was an understatement. There was no hymn-singing. The communion was like a bun-fight, with the priest being practically mobbed trying to give out the host, and to cap it all somebody had peed themselves.

The evidence of this was causing a small river to meander its way through the throng towards me. Its path was widening as it slowly pushed its way along the dark blue lino in my direction. I was sure it would reach me and continue on past me into the fireplace which I was standing beside. It couldn't go any further than this, so I was convinced I would get the blame for it. It stopped short of the fireplace and settled under my feet. Eyes were flashing from the congregation in front of me from the pool on the floor to my face, which was blood-red. Could this holiday get any worse?

The Mass ended, and eventually we all evacuated the makeshift chapel. I felt no better for the experience and faced another half hour's trek in the rain back along the beach to base camp. Hardly a single word was spoken on our return trip from Mass. I tried to lighten the mood by telling Stephen and a few of the lads about the piss-artist at church, and managed to get a bit of a response, but everybody was really depressed.

We continued the day by changing into any dry clothes we might have, and our wet clothes were strung inside the awning to drip dry. (What a hope!) There just wasn't anything to do in the rain. Johnnie was determined to make us hunt for our next meal of rabbit and equally, we were determined to refuse to hunt, or eat, the wretched creatures. A situation of stalemate was developing; even a hint of mutiny was detected by the bold Johnnie. He insisted we all bucked our ideas up and made the best of it.

We were given the choice of either staying in the bell tent for the rest of the day or we could go with him to fix set lines to catch fish from the incoming tide. Most of us opted for the former and concocted a fiendish plan to murder Johnnie and bury his body in the Drigg Dump among the contaminated waste from Sellafield, where it would never be discovered and we could say he went missing fixing the set lines and must have been drowned.

By the fourth day we were drawing lots for who should actually stick the knife in him, and lads were even volunteering. We'd had four days of practically starvation rations, except for breakfast, when we filled ourselves up with cornflakes and baked beans. The larder tent was full and we were being forced to hunt for these bloody rotten rabbits.

Shorty Connor was the first to crack. He cut a small slit in the canvas at the bottom of the back of the larder tent and plunged his hand in. He came into the bell tent with four tins of corned beef and two loaves of bread. We opened the corned beef and ripped bits of the meat off the solid lump with our fingers and gorged on the sweet meat and bread. Johnnie discovered the rip in the tent and the missing items of food and suspected poor Shorty straight away.

Without any further ado, he took him round the back of the larder tent and laid into him. We heard the screams and thought we would be next, but Johnnie didn't reappear. Poor wee Shorty slumped back into the bell tent with a tear-stained face and wouldn't admit to having had a beating.

From then on we all raided the larder tent and ate our fills of Spam, tinned pears, pink lint, beans and sausages, teacakes and all manner of goodies which had been intended for our use from day one. Johnnie had gone awol and this was the perfect opportunity to make a run for it. Stephen and me and four other pows made our way to Drigg railway station and caught a train to Whitehaven and a bus to Cleator Moor and home.

Mam nearly died when we walked in looking like we'd escaped from Auschwitz. Well, we felt we must have looked emaciated and poxy by now. She fed us and listened to our terrible tale of woe and sympathised with us for doing a runner and said he would have to face her when school started back on Monday, which he didn't have to do because Mam bottled out and said we would just have to go to school and see what happened.

About half of the group of lads on the trip had gone home by one means or another, and the remainder had stayed the full week, and on our return to school regaled us with tales of brilliant weather, camp fires and midnight feasts, a trip to Ravenglass and a boat trip off the sand banks. They'd had a visit to the gun range at Eskmeals and a trip on the Ratty to Eskdale, where Johnnie treated them all to tea and ice creams. The absconders were taken to task by Johnnie and told we would never be included in any future trips he planned. (There is a God.)

All's well that ends well.

CHAPTER 23
A VISIT TO WHITYHEAD FARM

Our visits to Whityhead Farm were rare and wonderful treats. Papa Heron got cock chickens for Christmas Day and Easter Sunday from his old mate, Charlie Weightman who lived at Whityhead, on the narrow winding road from Hale to Coldfell, about three miles from Egremont. It was a mixed farm; partly fell farm with sheep and dairy and a few taties and veg. They had pigs, banties, a few geese and ducks. There was an orchard with damson trees and walnut trees. A typical low fellside farm.

It was like taking a step back in time. The farmhouse and barns were as old as the hills and unchanged for a couple of hundred years. The farmhouse had slate floors and low oak beams and windows hardly big enough to let light in. It was steeped in Cumbrian history and tradition.

The old man himself wore knee-length corduroy breeches with hard black leather spats and hobnailed clogs, a waistcoat and collarless shirt which looked like it had been made from striped ticking. He spoke in a practically indecipherable Cumbrian dialect. He was well into hound trading; as was Papa, and the conversation was mostly hound crack. The two old men shared a mutual ease with each other.

We were always offered tea and homemade fruit cake, or scones and butter. The whole place had a Dickensian air about it; they were all very old-fashioned and unpretentious. The womenfolk, Charlie's wife and daughter-in-law were always busy plucking chickens and baking and gave us a warm welcome. The kitchen smelt of baking and silage and the ceiling hung with hams curing and 'smalls' drying. The whole place was a hive of activity.

In the scullery next to the kitchen was a small dairy with butter and cheeses on stone slabs and cold boxes made of wood and fine wire mesh. Half a dozen unplucked chickens strung together by the feet, hung from a meat hook from the ceiling near to the window.

Charlie would greet Papa with, 'What sec a fettle Stivven?'
And Papa would answer, 'I'm champion, Charlie, how's yerself?'

We'd be ushered in and the banter between Papa and the womenfolk would result in the women giggling and laughing in a very girlie manner, always calling Papa 'Mr 'Eron.' They were country folk and visitors were rare and relished when they arrived, especially ones who would be paying good money for at least a dozen cock chickens and a couple of hundred-weight of vegetables; always mixing business with pleasure.

On one occasion, Charlie was relating the saga of one of the farmhands who had had a 'skinful' of drink at the Hale pub and fell unconscious into the dyke on his way back to the farm. The labourer had said, 'How lang ah ligged int dyke I couldn't say. When I woke it were dawn and ah was liggin in amongst a lock a maudies.' (Moles). 'They'd med a gey, queer scraw in t' field.'

This was met by shrieks of laughter from the womenfolk, Charlie said, 'He's no' but a lad. As lang as it doesn't keep him frae his wark in t' byre, ah's nut bothered. He's sweetheartin' a la'al body frae Wilton. Mind, he likes gittin' round amang folk, Stivven.' This was followed by more shrieks of laughter.

'I says 'til him, "Thou wants to marry an auld maid wid a lock o' land." And he says, "Shed ha' to have thousands o' yackers, or I'd be married till a lock o' wark".' More hysterical laughter from the womenfolk.

'He'd better git her wed gey sharp, Stivven, what does thou say? Young folk! He's va'near din hissen' in.' Papa just laughed with them. It was all full of nudge, nudge, wink, wink, and lost on me because I couldn't understand a word he said, never mind understand what he meant.

'It's a gey lang time sen I did any liggin in any dykes Stivven, or any sec like doins on it,' said Charlie amid more fits of laughter from the womenfolk.

The pace of work on the farm seemed very slow, but constant. There always seemed time to 'down tools' and engage in a bit of crack. The work could wait; it would get done – if not today then tomorrow would do and without a doubt it seemed the work would be there forever. You could never get on top of it, so let it wait, and anyway, chances are there might not be another opportunity for company for days so enjoy it while you can. That was the impression I got.

They never spoke directly to us; it always seemed to be through Papa, 'Do you think t' la'al lads 'ud like a bit of heam-mead cake, Mr

'Eron?' Mrs Weightman would say. And we'd look at Papa with a very definite 'Yes' plastered all over our faces, but he would answer for us.

Yan sec like Saturday morning (you see how easy it is to pick it up), we'd called for our taties and eggs and there was a bit of a kerfuffle at the far end of the farmyard. The old bull was doing his stuff with one of the heifers. He apparently had a harem of some forty-odd females and this was *his busy time of year,* as Papa explained to us.

Old Charlie was in the thick of it, so to speak. The bull was getting a bit 'cheesed off' and making a lot of noise, with nostrils flared and much panting. He didn't seem to be able to hit his target, or maybe he'd been busy all morning and was losing his concentration; or maybe he wasn't that bothered whether or not he hit his target.

Papa said, 'He's probably ready for a sit down and a smoke.' (I think that was a joke.) So without hesitation or even a backward glance, Charlie waded in, got hold of the bull's 'teapot' with both hands (actually it was more like a roll of oil cloth) and hurled it as if he was tossing the caber into the desired receptacle. The young heifer responded with a slight squeal and after about three purposeful thrusts the bull dismounted and began to psyche himself up for the next one.

There seemed to be a queue building up of hopeful females in the yard next to where the bull was strutting his stuff. Charlie, after seeing Papa and us, gave instructions to his lad to 'Give the old bugger a drink of water and let him have a rest for half an hour till I talk to Stivven.' At that we followed Charlie into the farmhouse to receive our usual gaggle of greeting from the womenfolk.

Old Charlie's hands were like shovels and I can never remember him rushing to wash them before he tucked into his slab of fruit cake and his mug of tea. But he lived to a ripe old age and never seemed to take any harm, so maybe you can build up a resistance to muck if you eat enough of it.

We were never taught the facts of life by our parents, but being surrounded by animal procreation of one sort or another taught us the basics. Mind you the finer points of lovemaking would need to be improved upon when our turn came, because if we took any notice of Charlie's old bull we'd get short shrift from any prospective girlfriends. So there was a lot left to learn.

CHAPTER 24
THE FAIRIES' DEN

Just across the field from Whityhead Farm, in the middle distance between the farm and Cold Fell, stood a natural mound of rock surrounded by a perfect circle of Scots pines; Papa said it was where the fairies came to dance on Midsummer's Night. The trees had been planted hundreds of years ago to encourage the fairies to come back every year because they brought good luck.

We used to walk past the Fairy Glen on our walks with Papa to Matty Benn's Bridge, an old narrow stone packhorse bridge over the beck used over two hundred years ago for mules carting the slate from the old quarry to be made into roofing slates . It was also used to carry the coffins from the old farmstead high on the fell side for burial at Ponsonby or Hale and was known as the 'Coffin Road'.

There was a popular hound trail held on these back fells regularly during the summer months, and Papa used to take us with him sometimes, except when he was doing his more serious betting. A lot of money changed hands at the trails and Papa was well-known for his heavy betting on these occasions. I think it was his only vice, and I'm sure Nana didn't know how much he won and lost, but it was his passion and he followed the trails all over the county, taking with him a car full of his loyal followers and hangers-on to every meeting.

He had a pair of German First World War binoculars which he used to watch for the hounds to appear over the distant fells. As soon as he spotted the first hound he'd make his assessment of the field and place his final bet. Once the dogs came into reasonable view the betting would stop and the punters would hope for the best. That's where Papa met old Charlie Wheatman and many of the farmers who all knew him by name. I think there was a side to Papa Heron I knew nothing about, but he was the best grandfather in the world.

CHAPTER 25
THE BLACK WOOD (BROKEN LAND)

Strictly speaking, the Black Wood was out of range, but 'nothing ventured, nothing gained' and these expeditions were never really carefully planned. The vague outline of the day's walking was to go to broken land, try and catch some tiddlers, then make our way up to Black How Farm onto the fell road, up through the deer fields, into the third wood, cross over the Reservoir Field and into the Black Wood where we would light a fire. Actually, that sounds pretty comprehensive, but there was sure to be a change of plan midway, or somebody's mother would send one of the big lads after us on a bike and scupper the whole expedition. We usually hid in the dyke when we saw a big lad on a bike in the distance.

Somehow today I had a gut feeling we'd make it to the Black Wood where I'd only managed to walk to once before, with Joe Farren, the year before. We'd gone by Joe Scrugham's Snagger Field, a direct line between the Iron Bridge and the Fell Road. Joe knew all the best rose-hip bushes and was in line for a third rose-hip badge and a possible trip to the Pontefract Factory, so some serious picking was needed; heads down and no talking was the order of the day that day.

It was a long way but there was no hurry; we had all day. Armed with a bottle of water, some Spam sandwiches, an apple and an empty jam jar to catch the tiddlers in, we set off; our Stephen, Robert Looney, Edward Fitzpatrick, Raymond Graham and myself (all cousins). We had to leave Cleator Village via the Beck Bridge at the bottom of Kiln Brow. You see, Cleator Village was an island, cut off on the west side by the Lonnie Beck and the east side by Hen Beck (the River Ehen) which separates the low-lying coastal strip from the foothills of the Lake District.

The west side of Cleator Village had soft rolling countryside, with the cricket field and cock ring, the old disused mine workings and slag banks, the railway embankments and sewage works, the Red Hill and Lonny Beck. It had seen better days, but once you crossed the Beck Bridge to the east side of the village, the scenery changed dramatically.

Immediately ahead of you was Dent mountain, only just scraping through as a mountain, because some of the locals argued that if it wasn't for the stone cairns at the top of Dent, put there to guide the shepherds in the fog, Dent wasn't actually 1000ft high, therefore disqualifying it from the full status of a mountain.

This led to many an argument after closing time at the Miller's Inn. Some staunch, loyal supporters of Dent Mountain were prepared to fight to uphold the mountain status. To be honest it didn't really look like a mountain to me. It had no overhanging crags or jutting out rocks. It was just round and smooth, completely covered in grass and bracken except for the occasional wood, the Black Wood included. Papa Heron took all the grandchildren to the top of it on his 70th birthday. The Black Wood was just a few hundred yards from the bottom, quite a steep climb. Our walk would traverse across the Deer Fields from the third wood, rather than go straight up from Nook Farm.

It was a walk of about a quarter of a mile between the Beck Bridge and Broken Land which was the name of the man-made lake where we were going to catch our tiddlers. All sorts of stories abounded about the origins of the Broken Land. Some people said it had been a quarry which had flooded and that there were houses at the bottom of it and people were living in them when the beck broke its banks and started to flood the quarry. It was even said that some people were drowned in their beds and some managed to scramble to the top before the waters swallowed them up.

It was also said that it was bottomless. Lots of local ponds were bottomless because they were the top section of a disused pit which went almost a mile underground. This was the case with Broken Land. In fact, it had been a series of pits all bunched together and the pit heads were very near the beck edge.

The beck had been re-routed away from the pits and concrete channels were formed to take the flow of the beck away from the shafts and where the River Ehen and the Lonny Beck met, a huge reinforced double concrete channel had been formed – still visible to this day with huge cracks in it along its length of some five or six hundred yards.

When the pits were worked out they flooded and all collapsed into each other to form a huge crater which filled with water and was known to us as Broken Land; more recently renamed Longlands Lake, which eventually formed its own ecosystem of fish, frogs, newts, tiddlers, bird life and plant life.

The name Broken Land didn't seem to describe what was there at the time, but would better fit the description of the scene when the pits were working some thirty years earlier. I knew some old men in the village who had worked at the pits so it wasn't so long ago.

The remains of at least three old bridge stations were visible, scattered haphazardly along the length of the river bank at this point which would have been opposite the pit heads, one of the bridges was opposite the old foundry and forge which were on the Cleator side of the beck and were recently closed down.

I felt I'd missed out on the madness and activity of the mining era, which must have been a very exciting time; a bit like El Dorado and the gold rushes of the Wild West. It had all been happening here and I could still feel the energy it had generated and the heroic and romantic images it threw up at me were inspirational.

There was a partly derelict ammunition shed built of sandstone walls and an arched brick roof made to withstand an accidental dynamite explosion, and a sandstone bulkhead on the edge of the water line which must have been part of a huge pulley system or conveyor belt, driven by powerful steam engines. Little bits of evidence of these machines were strewn across a wide area and our imagination ran riot when we happened upon them.

The riverside walk from the Beck Bridge to the Dub (the deep pool near Broken Land where we used to swim) was fenced off with a cast iron fence which looked like long vertical spears with sharp points on the end of them. Old Mr Todhunter had a garden between the beck and the fence where he kept pigs and goats. He was a bit of a mystery man. His name comes from the old Cumbrian name for a fox (a Todd), hence Todhunter. He lived in the old Mission Rooms on Kiln Brow.

A bit further downstream, a gate allowed access to an area we called the weir, although there wasn't any evidence of a weir at that time, just a sheltered gravel beach which was good for sunbathing and playing ducks and drakes.

Just before the Dub was a private bridge, a narrow cast iron suspension footbridge which provided access to the fields beyond from Dr Henry's house. It had a stout iron gate at this end which was always locked. I never saw anyone use it but it looked very ostentatious. It must have cost a fortune to build. A number of old houses were built here along the beck edge, probably to do with the Foundry and Forge, hence the abundance of cast iron fencing and the footbridge.

The object of the visit to Broken Land was to catch tiddlers and the shallow beach on the north side of the lake provided us with a jam jar full in a matter of half an hour or so. Our Stephen was good at catching tiddlers, but Raymond Graham hadn't the patience; he was more inclined to wander on ahead on his own all the time.

In fact, Auntie Lily used to threaten us not to come back without him, but we couldn't always keep track of him and more often than not he'd go missing early into most of our expeditions – this one being no exception. The two young cousins Edward and Robert were happy to tag along and were contented to listen to Stephen and me. We would tell them stories about the terrible flood and all the screaming children trying to scramble out of the crater. They didn't stray very far from our sides.

We paddled in the clear water up to our knees for about an hour and we were ready for our bait. So we sat in the bullrushes at the edge of the lake and soaked up the sun and made up the most ridiculous and unbelievable stories about Rob Roy and Bonnie Prince Charlie having camped here on their way to the Scottish Borders and the Battle of Culloden. In fact, we found an old piece of tartan rag in the reeds which must have come from a kilt, so how much proof do you need? That, rather conveniently, proved our stories to be correct.

The wee lads were a bit tired now so a bit of gentle encouragement and a short sharp shock would motivate them to start the next stage of our journey to the Black Wood. Stephen spotted a pair of water rats making their way over to our discarded bread crusts, so we all took off like a shot, for fear of being bitten by them and the 'Safari' was on the move again. We'd pick the petals off a dandelion and say, *'She loves me, she loves me not, she loves me, she loves me not,* until the last petal fell to the ground and she either loved me or loved me not, whoever she was.

By now we were half way up the cobbled stoned lonning, heading to Black How and Nook Farms, which was quite steep. The first straight stretch seemed to go on forever and because of the high hedges on both sides, it was a bit stifling and a hard pull up for the young cousins. Edward complained because he always complained, but Robert was uncomplaining and stoic in his attempt to get to the end of the lonning where the promise of a sit down and a nice red apple kept him going.

Raymond was still nowhere to be seen, but he'd turn up sooner or later, no doubt. Black How Farm was in sight and the only way through the farmyard was through six inches of sloppy cow clap. We tip-toed through the slurry and managed to completely cover our black sandshoes and socks in the stinky stuff.

On the opposite side of the Fell Road through the farmyard, we eventually reached the sheep dipper and the high iron fence which surrounded the Deer Park below the third wood. These fences had been put up some hundred years earlier to keep the deer contained; they were farmed to provide venison for the gentry at the Flosh and Ehen Hall. They were just a relic of a former era now and were more than adequate to keep in the sheep which occupied these low-lying fields today.

We just skirted round the third wood on our way to the reservoir. This is an ancient wood, not like the carefully manicured larch and scotch pine plantations planted by the Forestry Commission. It had huge oaks and sycamores, mountain ash and holly trees. Under the high canopy you find the ground elder and bluebells and primroses. The mosses cover the rocks like soft cushions. The magic mushrooms and wild garlic give a pungent smell when you brush past them. Its what most of the lowlands must have been covered with before the forests were felled for firewood in the olden days. We have coal now and no need for firewood any longer.

The lads were about all in by now, so to spur them on I promised them a swim in the reservoir when we got to it, which would be soon. Robert spotted a figure in the distance hiding behind one of the pillars of the bottom wall of the reservoir, so we were all on our guard whilst crossing the Deer Park, the last leg of our journey.

Stephen said, 'It looked like the Witch of Nanny Catch,' but he was just scare-mongering to frighten the young lads and make himself seem brave, surging ahead. The figure seemed to have disappeared, so maybe it was just the way the light had caught the high walls. The shadows could play tricks with you.

The reservoir had been built by the Victorian stone masons for the village of Cleator and funded by the Ainsworths and Lowthers who owned most of the property in Cleator. It was built to resemble a castle with corner turrets and what looked like a drawbridge, but was in fact the filtration plant which consisted of a series of iron grilles to keep the deer and grouse from going into the pipes. It had high walls on three sides and was built into the natural stone formation.

It was red-hot by now and we were all a bit shattered when we finally arrived. We just lay down on the flat grass area beside the water. The wee lads were pestering to have the swim I'd promised them so I could see no harm as long as Stephen and me kept a good eye on them and anyhow we could all swim. So we peeled off down to the buff and Stephen dived in first, followed by me, and after we surfaced and assured the lads it wasn't cold at all (God forgive us), they jumped in and could hardly get their breath when they popped back up, both saying 'it's dead warm' and shivering at the same time!

The steps leading to the filtration grilles went down some six feet or so and it was great to walk down them and disappear below water level, The old reservoir hadn't been used since Victorian times and the pipes heading from it to the water system below were blocked off. The Water Board hadn't visited it for years because it wasn't needed any more. Maybe it didn't even belong to the Water Board.

Robert had a turn at walking down the steps and immediately shot back up screaming 'There's something down there!' He was terrified and shaking.

Stephen said, 'Don't be daft, man, what do you mean?'

Robert blurted out, 'You go and have a look, if you don't believe me. There's something in a sack near the grilles, I saw it.'

I asked, 'What did it look like, Rob?'

'It looked like a wee babby. I could see its head sticking out of the sack.'

He'd definitely seen something to put him in such a state. Stephen said, 'I'm not going down, Sean, you have a look.' The thought of finding a wee babby in a sack at the bottom of the steps terrified me, but someone had to take a look, so I walked round to the steps and looked hard into the water which was quite clear at the surface, but the grilles could only be seen from under the water because it was so deep and black.

I put my face to the surface of the water, dipped my head in and opened my eyes. I brought my head out fast. I could definitely see a sack or an old blanket or something and yes, I could see what looked like a head sticking out of it. I felt sick. I couldn't believe we'd found a babby's body. Stephen said, 'Well, what did you see?' Just then a huge cobble landed right beside us, it was that bloody Raymond Graham, he'd beaten us to the reservoir and was just waiting his chance to get us all together and soak us.

Stephen chased after him and caught him in the bracken at the top end of the reservoir and we all dragged him to the edge of the water and threw him in fully clothed. This had taken our minds off the dead babby momentarily, but as soon as Raymond surfaced Stephen told him to dive down and see what was at the bottom of the steps – which he did. He was the strongest swimmer of the group and could dive and stay under water for ages. He seemed to be down forever.

We were all standing spellbound, waiting for him to resurface. When he eventually did he had his hands covered in slimy wool. Just seconds after he resurfaced, even before he got his breath back, the hideous corpse of a dead sheep surfaced with him. We all stepped back and could see the dead sheep with the head of its lamb sticking out of its rear end. It looked hideous. The poor old thing must have been having a bad time lambing and fallen into the water. Raymond said it was wedged into the grilles with a log over its back. What a terrible death to suffer, but thank God it wasn't a wee babby.

We took ten minutes or so to recover from the shock and listened to Raymond's story about having to wait for nearly an hour to get us all together before he hurled his cobble. We decided we'd wasted enough time; we needed to press on with the last quarter of a mile across the Deer Field and so we set off once again.

The Black Wood loomed up like some menacing cloud and the darkness under its low canopy took a bit of adjusting to. The wee lads were a bit afraid of the spooky wind noises, whistling through the dense blackness, but once you got used to the semi-darkness, it was very exciting. The bottom six feet or so of the larch trees were bare and the forest floor was completely covered in a bed of soft pine needles.

We scrambled up the first steep slope to a flat section of wood and started to gather up some small fallen branches. Once we'd gathered enough for our fire, we collected some dry pine needles and dead bracken and formed the fire.

We had found a slightly more open section of the wood for our campfire so as to minimise the possibility of causing a forest fire and I struck the first match. The bracken caught straight away and the tinder dry branches soon became alight. This was great we could flee the heat from the burning branches and as soon as the smoke settled down we were all content to watch the red glow and reflect on the day's adventures.

Raymond was raging because he'd brought a cinnamon stick for us to smoke, but he'd had to dry it out first because it had been in his shirt pocket when we threw him in the reservoir. After a short while, the cinnamon stick was dry enough to light, so we all took it in turns to have a drag and it tasted really good once you got used to the thick brown smoke. Raymond inhaled and nearly choked himself, so the rest of us gave it a miss.

Raymond had hung his shorts and shirt over a branch beside the fire to dry and the wee lads set about gathering more dead wood. Edward had brought a strip of lead he found in his Dad's hut and an empty shoe polish tin, so I carefully folded the strip of lead into the tin and placed it into the embers of the fire, it only took a couple of minutes to melt. So, as soon as it was liquid, I lifted it off between two sticks and poured little drops of lead onto the flat stones near the fire.

As soon as the lead started to set I poked a small thin twig into one end of each blob and let it completely harden. This would leave a hole in the lead to thread the catgut through, so we could use them as sinkers for our fishing lines. I gathered about ten or so up, pulled the twigs out and put them back into the polish tin to use at a later date. We must have been sitting around for at least an hour by now and strange noises were filtering through the wood like ghostly voices.

Then a very definite voice could be heard shouting and getting nearer to where we were sitting. We all shot off in different directions and eventually met up in a clearing near the top of the wood, Raymond minus his shirt and shorts, shivering in his damp underpants. We'd caused a bit of a sensation, because apparently the farmer had seen the plumes of smoke filtering through the treetops and must have thought the wood was on fire. He and two of the farm hands had raced up into the wood either to try and put it out or find out who was responsible.

Suddenly, we heard the bells of the fire engine and we knew we were in deep trouble. I took charge at this point and a sudden rush of adrenaline made it quite clear to me we had to go to ground and wait this one out, because I knew if we got caught it would be Borstal for Steve, Ray and me. We hadn't intended to burn the wood down and the fire was out of the range of the main trees, but no-one would believe us, so very quietly we found a thick area of high bracken and hid for what seemed like hours in complete silence.

Before very long the farmers were nearby and we could clearly hear their talking. One of them was saying, 'They must still be in the wood, and when I catch them I'll lay into them 'til they bleed.' We were petrified. Robert and Edward were quietly crying, Raymond was threatening to kill them if they didn't shut up. So their sobs died down and we stayed still for at least an hour, in fact it was nearly dark and we knew half of Cleator would be out looking for us if we didn't turn up soon.

Stephen said, 'Well make a break for it up the top of the wood towards Egremont and back down to Nook Farm and back home.' Once we got to the top of the wood it was all downhill and we ran the whole way home without stopping. Poor Raymond was still in his underpants and that was going to take some explaining. He hid in the wood at the bottom of Kiln Brow and I sneaked back to our house, casually walked upstairs and threw a pair of spare shorts and a shirt Raymond had brought with him for the weekend from the bedroom window to Stephen, who was waiting in the garden. He picked them up and we both raced back to Kiln Brow to find Raymond nearly suffering from hypothermia.

The big problem was the wee cousins They should have been home hours ago and Auntie Mary and Auntie Maggie had been to our house looking for them. I took Robert back home and Stephen took Edward and both of us got a 'flea in our ear' for keeping them out so late.

We stuck to our pre-rehearsed story about playing on the raft on

Broken Land and hadn't realised the time. Now, if the youngsters don't 'blow our gaffe' we could get away with it, but, by tomorrow, the crack will be out about the fire and the Police will be asking questions. Mam wasn't best pleased about us keeping the wee lads out so late and Dad said it would be the belt for us next time we did anything like it. God help us if they find out about the fire. Raymond would have to explain about the missing clothes when he got back home but *so far so good*.

We all ate our supper in almost complete silence. Dad said, 'What's wrong with you lads, has the cat got your tongues?'

And Mam said, 'Leave them alone, Jay, they're tired out. They've been away since nine o'clock this morning and they just need their beds.'

Needless to say, we hardly slept a wink – only nine hours or so. The next morning we had to be wakened for ten o'clock Mass. Father O'Connell gave a sermon on being honest and the dangers of dying in mortal sin. I felt like shit for the rest of the day.

The crack had got out and Joe Graham's shop was bursting with stories about the farmer chasing two big lads half way up Dent and watched them going towards Uldale Bottom. I don't know who the hell they could have been. The fire engine hadn't been needed, but the Police had some clothes that had been left by the lads and would be making enquiries. Joe said, 'The whole wood could have gone up. What the hell gets into kids these days?'

Mam asked us if we'd seen anything of the fire when we were at Broken Land and Stephen said, 'We heard the fire engine, but that's all.' Why Raymond's clothes were never missed by Auntie Lily and Mam I'll never know, but Raymond was never asked about them so we'd got away with it all, swearing never to light a fire near a wood again, *but what a great day it had been!*

CHAPTER 26
ENNERDALE RURAL DISTRICT COUNCIL

The Flosh was the home of Ennerdale Rural District Council. It was a very grand mansion built by the Ainsworths. It was in fact their country seat, and commanded a fabulous view over Dent. The grounds had been laid out to include a woodland walk, lawn terraces and a first class croquet lawn.

The grounds were maintained by Ennerdale Rural District Council for the use of the people of Cleator as a park. They had 'Keep off the Grass' signs everywhere. Part of the grounds had a small play area with a carousel and a few swings. The yews were clipped like statues and the whole place had an air of grandeur about it. There was a rose arbour and formal flowerbeds and the lawns were immaculately kept.

Two full-time gardeners were employed and they had magnificent greenhouses where they raised all their own bedding plants. The older gardener was a bit of an old crab and didn't like kids. We used to go in the park on our bikes or bogies and he used to chase us if we touched any of the grass verges with our tyres.

They finished work at five o'clock and we could really let our hair down then, riding up and down the sandstone steps leading to the croquet lawn, hiding in the hollowed-out yews and swinging in the trees. As long as we didn't make too much noise and let Uncle Billy hear us. Uncle Billy, Dad's brother and his wife, Auntie Claire, were caretakers of the Flosh; they lived in a flat in the big house. They had two children then, Gerard and Elizabeth. Gregory came a bit later.

Stephen and me used to go to play with Gerard after school, and we could roam freely round the Council offices. The front door was a wonderful glass swing door and we used to get inside it and run round as fast as we could go. The air used to rush out of the opening every time we passed and the sound was terrifying. The long hallway was very ornately decorated with gold leaf on the ceiling and cornices and the warm oak doors and skirtings were highly polished.

The hall had a white marble fire-grate and a huge plush couch that must have been twenty feet long. We used to take our shoes off and bounce from one end of it to the other. It was sprung like a trampoline. We weren't allowed into the Council Chambers themselves, but now and again Uncle Billy would leave the door open when he had been dusting and we would sneak in.

It was very like a courtroom with a huge oak table and twenty or so seats around it. There were a couple of elevated seats like thrones and dozens of oil paintings of former Lord Mayors and dignitaries; it was like another world. Our favourite room was the Drawing Office. This was upstairs in what would have been the master bedroom. It had the most fabulous view over to Dent and Sylverston's factory where they used to make army uniforms. The factory was in the style of a Lancashire cotton mill, about four storeys high, built of well-dressed sandstone with hundreds of huge sliding sash windows.

The wall facing the Flosh had a cast iron fire escape crossing it from the top to the bottom with doors opening on to each level. The women who worked at the mill used to have their bait on the fire escape on sunny days. We could see them when we were coming home from school, we used to wave at them the way you used to wave at a passing train. There was something quite poignant and sad the way they waved back; almost like prisoners waving behind their prison bars.

Actually, the Mill, as we called it, was built by the Ainsworths in the nineteenth century, probably to make cotton and I suspect it was the reason for their deserting the Flosh, because of its close proximity to the big house. The Ainsworths had a private road built to take the family by horse-drawn carriage from the Flosh to Whitehaven. Some of the road still exists.

It went across the field from the front of the Flosh, through a gate to Jacktrees Road, through another gate across the field leading to the cricket field over an iron bridge across the Lonny Beck on to Moor Row, where the family would catch the train to London. What about that? Your very own private road complete with bridges. What opulence! There were a series of lodge houses along the route and a bell system rang from one lodge house to the next to let the lodge keepers know when to open the gates for the Ainsworths' carriages.

One of the rooms in the Flosh had the words 'Housing Officer, Mr Buttery' on it and I had seen Mr Buttery on the backs at Cleator. People either loved or hated him. He was the man with the power to decide whether you got re-housed or not. Now, at that particular time loads of houses were in a bad state of repair and many had been declared uninhabitable. *Condemned* was the buzzword.

Everybody wanted their rented houses condemned so they could move into one of the new Council houses being built at Cleator Moor. It went on a points system; depending on how many children you had, what amenities or lack of them you had and sometimes even if you didn't want to leave your house, Buttery was the man who said 'yea' or 'nay'. He had to inspect the old houses so he wasn't always well received.

The Drawing Office had huge drawing boards with graph paper and plans pinned to them and Uncle Billy used to let us draw on the empty drawing boards with coloured pens and draughtsmen's pencils. The offices were connected with a telephone intercom and we used to phone each other from office to office. As I said before, as long as we didn't make too much noise Uncle Billy didn't mind. He used to play tricks on us like pretending cupboards were haunted and jumping out on us.

I found myself preoccupied with the view over Dent from these windows and thought how strange that this building had once been occupied by a family. I imagined children playing in the garden as we often did and convinced myself I could see a little girl standing very still beside one of the clipped yews. She was wearing a long white dress with black boots and she seemed to be distressed in some way; almost as if she was fixed to the spot.

I was certain she would race off across the lawns and I'd be able to get a good look at her. I could hear far away the sound of bells and noticed that the little girl wasn't in fact a little girl, but a white painted beehive further into the wood than I thought I'd seen it at first and the distant bells was in fact the office door bell being pressed by my cousin Elizabeth who had been sent to fetch me for my tea. I wish I hadn't been disturbed, because I'm convinced I was witnessing something from a very long time ago and I'd just been cheated out of an amazing experience.

This place has its ghosts and I'm very receptive to their messages. Next time I come to play with Gerard, I'm going to get locked in the cellars and I'm bound to witness some strange happenings; I hope. I got a dressing down from Auntie Claire for disappearing and warned not to go off on my own again. You see, there are strange goings-on in this house and Auntie Claire was trying to protect me from them.

CHAPTER 27
AUNTY BETTY

My best mate of all time was Thomas, Thomas Osowski. His father, Felix, was Polish, his mother, Antoinette, (née Kennedy – very important) was of Irish descent and of course her grandfather was the famous Tom Kennedy of Cumberland and Westmorland wrestling fame.

Antoinette was a lady in the true sense of the word and over the years became my soul mate, God bless her.

They met in Blackpool just after the war. Antoinette was working as a secretary and Felix, a tall, dark handsome man, had landed in England after fighting in the Polish army against Hitler. His country was devastated, most of the family killed and the rest scattered in all directions.

Antoinette should have been born a Polish princess; she had the air of aristocracy about her and she was a truly gentle woman. Although her grandfather was a wrestler, her mother's family were very gentle, middle-class people; mostly school teachers, intellectuals and scholars. Fascinating people to me because they were so very different from my own down-to-earth working-class family.

Thomas was different from my other mates. He used words like bored and *incidentally* and wasn't embarrassed to express himself. We became friends for life. He had four sisters and one brother, and, despite the numbers, I was invited to spend two weeks holiday with them at Nethertown in a very small caravan. His mother used the philosophy that if you've got six kids, one extra didn't make any difference.

Katherine was the youngest, just a baby. We were all in bed and it was early morning, and Katherine was awake, she had a 'sniffy' - a garment she used to sniff, a sort of comforter. Unfortunately, it was an old pair of knickers; she trailed them round everywhere with her. Antoinette couldn't get them off her.

It was a bit like the 'Waltons' in a caravan. We were all tops and tails and, of course, every sound carried in the small space. Katherine decided she wanted her 'sniffy'. She couldn't find it, so she started: 'I want me knickers. I want me knickers. I want me knickers.' Now,

Antoinette was peace itself, rarely got angry and took life just as it came. She answered 'Alright, darling, I know,' half asleep herself. Katherine continued her chant for several more minutes and she continued to sympathise with her but made no attempt to get her 'sniffy'.

This continued on similar lines for about half an hour. Nobody except me seemed to be awake. Then out of the blue Thomas screamed, 'For Christ's sake, give her her bloody knickers, will you?'

Well Antoinette, quiet and demure as she was, shot up in bed and said, 'Thomas, how dare you use such language. That's blasphemy. Youll have to go to confession.'

He replied, 'I'll go to bloody confession, but for God's sake, give her her knickers, so we can all get some sleep.'

Thomas' Aunty Betty, a rather large lady, sweet-natured, a bit wistful and distant but very caring, absolutely adored Antoinette's children. She married late in life, meeting her husband on a pilgrimage to Lourdes and after only two years he was killed in a road accident in Blackpool. They had no children of their own.

She seemed very happy living with her two elderly aunts, Auntie Katie and Auntie Claire. She was to visit us in the caravan that day. Everybody was excited, because Auntie Betty always brought loads of presents and goodies and things. She was to arrive by taxi. Ada Adams always drove Betty wherever she went, and she seemed to travel everywhere by taxi.

For some reason she was late and should have been here at noon. It was now 2.15 pm and she hadn't arrived. Antoinette was worried. She decided she'd go to the phone box in the village and give Ada Adams a ring. Ada answered and told her she'd dropped Auntie Betty off at Thornhill at 11.45 am. She had decided she'd have a nice walk, Ada had said. This was Betty you see, no real grasp of how far Thornhill was from Nethertown, and hadn't considered the inconvenience she'd cause, not to mention the worry, her being three hours late for lunch.

Antoinette was furious. She said, 'This is typical of our Betty, no idea we might be worried out of our minds.' Betty's larger than life frame appeared like a mirage through the heat haze bouncing up from the tarmac as she struggled along the Nethertown road, loaded with large shopping bags and dozens of brown paper carrier bags.

To give some idea of the geography of the place for those who aren't familiar with the area, Cleator to Nethertown via Egremont is about six miles, turning due west at Egremont. Cleator to Thornhill is about five miles turning due south at Egremont, not exactly on route, you might say.

Antoinette said, 'If she wanted a walk why didn't she get Ada to drop her off at Middletown, just about a mile away; but still she'd have all sorts to carry. Oh, I don't understand.'

As it turned out poor Auntie Betty wasn't sure how far away Thornhill was from Nethertown, she thought she'd get a better view of the sea, and it was probably about a good mile to walk. Wrong! Thornhill to Nethertown through Braystones must be three to four miles. She was absolutely shattered. Poor Betty and poor Antoinette.

She forgot her anger the minute she saw the state Betty was in. Her hair was soaking with sweat and her face was like a turkey cock. Cups of tea and dishes of cold water and Eau de Cologne were administered for the next two hours until Betty composed herself. What an ordeal for the poor woman (the walk I mean, not the cups of tea etc.).

Betty returned home by taxi, courtesy of Ada Adams about eight o'clock in the evening, promising to return the next morning for a full day, no walking she promised. This she duly did.

The carrier bags she had brought the day before were as we all thought, full of goodies. Toys for the kids, buckets and spades, metal spades with wooden handles, plasticine in case it rained, colouring books, pencils, drawing pads and a huge kite with a ball of string. The shopping bag had pork pies, tins of salmon, crisps, Dent lemonade and a flask full of Hartley's ice-cream – we ate that straight away – roast ham, four loaves of bread and God knows what else. She loved her food did Betty, and, of course, she shared it with everybody.

It was another hot day, Betty said it was ideal for the kite because there was a good breeze, so we headed for the cliff tops, Betty included. To get to the cliff tops we had to go through Nethertown village, past Mr Wallace's shop and the Tourist Hotel Pub, past Tony Steel's farm and Mossop's Farm and another farm, all of which had their farmhouses in a sort of circle next door to each other leaving a village green in the centre.

Down the concrete road made by the army during the war to serve the army base at Nethertown, the remains of which were still visible then, bits of buildings all in facing brick, very utility looking and sinister. Over the railway bridge, turn right, past all the wooden bungalows, built by locals to spend the long hot summer holidays in. Some looked as if a gust of wind would blow them away, others looked quite sturdy, reinforced with asbestos sheeting and corrugated steel roof. Somehow the aesthetic quality of the building was diminished as the new age technology progressed in building materials, not a fact generally admitted then, I suppose people were just grateful to have some materials they could afford to buy.

We finally arrived at the cliff top. What a view! To the left was Sellafield and Seascale and beyond the sand dunes at Drigg and Ravenglass, all perfectly visible. Immediately in front of us is the Isle of Man, like a distant volcanic island. Then sweeping round to the right, the bottom end of Scotland, just visible, the beautiful Galloway coast, the Solway Firth and the stately St Bees head. Moving back nearer towards us, Calderton and Nethertown Station. The station house seemed to be built on an outcrop of land looking from here as if when the tide is in it will be completely surrounded by sea.

Just below is the beach, quite a lot of sand and lots of pools and rocks to catch crabs and pick covens and flithers. Then my favourite place in the entire universe, the breakwater, formed in a square to throw the tide away from the railway line. Because of its shape it made a perfect swimming pool. The tide filled it twice a day so it never became stagnant. It was about three feet deep at the deepest, so quite safe to swim in for us kids.

Betty hurled the kite in the air and like a huge eagle it soared to the end of the string which Betty held very firmly in her hand. She continued to hold the string and adamantly resisted all our calls to 'Let me have a go, Auntie Betty.' You see, Betty hadn't held a kite since she was a child and was absolutely entranced in the sense of power and control she had over its movements as she pulled the string and made it dip and soar back up with real skill. She was mesmerised.

We continued to beg her to let us have a go, but no, she didn't seem to hear us at all. Now and again she'd say, 'Yes, pet, in a little while. Auntie's enjoying herself. Why don't you go and have a swim?' She could have been saying, 'Why don't you go and play on the railway line?' for all she cared at that moment. She was in bliss. Thomas and me thought this was hysterical, and we thought 'Good old Auntie Betty, she's one of us.'

So we left Auntie Betty in ecstasy and followed the footpath down the railway line to the breakwater, where we had arranged, or should I say Betty had arranged to meet Antoinette. Antoinette was not even slightly surprised when we arrived without Betty. She said, 'Oh, you know our Betty loves kites. When she was a little girl she spent hours up the big hill with her kite.' Hence the amazing skill she still had.

The edge of the breakwater was very round and smooth, ground down with years of pounding from the tide. It was made of stone covered with concrete and reflected the sun. You couldn't lie down on it when the sun had been on it for a few hours. Such were the conditions that day.

Antoinette had made dozens of salmon sandwiches and Betty's crisps and lemonade were an absolute treat. The smell of the sea and salt on our lips from swimming in the tide, the heat of the sun and my perfect surrogate family. How happy I was.

Betty was still visible on the cliff tops, even some three hours later. Antoinette said, 'She'll be back soon. She's bound to be hungry by now.' Those words had such depth of feeling. Sure enough, minutes later Betty arrived with a smile on her face the likes of which I have never seen since.

She ate very birdlike, and satisfied herself quite soon, then announced, to Antoinette's horror and Thomas' and my delight, she was going for a swim.

'But you haven't got a bathing costume,' Antoinette begged.

'No, dear. I'll have to go in as I am.' Betty replied.

'But you can't dear. You just can't,' said Antoinette, 'What will people think?' as she looked all around to see how many people were about. Well, it wasn't exactly the south pier at Blackpool, but it was quite busy for Nethertown. There must have been about twenty people scattered over a mile stretch of beach. Antoinette was horrified, but, in spite of the fact that, as Antoinette pointed out, she would have to sit in her dress until it dried, she was determined. She had made up her mind and nothing was going to stop her.

She slowly made her way across the rocks until she got to the lagoon left by the tide on its way out. She launched herself immediately and swam around the lagoon like a galleon in full sail. God love her she was having the time of her life. After about an hour, she returned up the beach soaked to the pelt literally. Talk about a wet tee-shirt competition, she'd have walked away with it had there been one that day.

Antoinette was beside herself. 'For goodness' sake, Betty, dear, sit down and cover yourself up,' she said. 'You're embarrassing the boys.' Not at all. We thought this was the funniest thing we'd seen since Eunice Horricks' breast flopped out through the side of her pinny when she was skipping with the lasses on Cleator backs last summer. She just picked it up and stuck it back and carried on skipping, to the delight of Roy Hodgson and Trevor Palmer, who cheered her on. What a laugh! Talk about salad days.

Auntie Betty lived with her two elderly Aunts and the two old Aunts were a throwback from Victorian days. Auntie Katie looked quite modern, but was steeped in the past. Memories of colonial days in Kimberly, her husband had been a miner in the South African gold mines. They had lived the high life in Cape Town and Johannesburg with black servants and lackeys to do every mortal thing for them. Actually, nothing much had changed. Auntie Betty had replaced a staff of about ten servants, but did the job admirably.

Katie had lost an eye through cancer and didn't always wear her dark glasses. This could be a bit shocking if you weren't expecting it. Auntie Claire was a retired school teacher and very kindly and softly spoken.

When they became too much for Auntie Betty they went to a nursing home, The Little Sisters of the Poor in Carlisle. Auntie Betty would dutifully get the train to Carlisle on Saturday morning, book into the Crown and Mitre Hotel for her overnight stay and get a taxi to Botchergate, the Little Sisters home for the elderly. The family had given generously over a lifetime to The Little Sisters of the Poor, who were always well-received, Cleator Moor being a large Catholic community; so it was time to collect, as it were, for the

Aunties.

I don't know how much it cost in those days to go into a Nursing Home like that, but if you had money you were expected to pay, and the old Aunties would have money.

Betty's visits were quite fraught because I remember her telling Antoinette that one of the sisters always had a birthday or something every week, and they asked her for a donation. It was either Sister Immaculata had her sixtieth birthday, would you like to make a donation, or Sister Scholastica is going to Rome on Wednesday to have an audience with the Blessed Father, and a generous donation would be very helpful. Betty swallowed it every time and gave with a very good grace, God forgive them.

Of course, between her train fare, bed and breakfast and evening meal at the Crown and Mitre, and her taxis around town, and her generous donation to the Little Sisters, not to mention her gifts of chocolate, scented soaps and paper hankies for the Aunties, it must have cost her a bomb. As it happened, their stay at the Little Sisters was quite short-lived because Auntie Betty received a telegram from the Sisters one morning saying the Aunties had been transferred to the Garlands Hospital and she should visit them there, which she did.

The Garlands was a hospital for the mentally ill, and Betty discovered that the Sisters had made the Aunties clean toilets and do menial jobs, which they weren't used to and which they had objected to, hence their departure. Both of them said the Garlands was much nicer than the Sisters of the Poor, they quite liked it here.

Thomas and me visited Auntie Betty just after the Sisters took the aunts into care, because Thomas was concerned that Auntie Betty would be lonely being suddenly on her own. She must have had very mixed feelings about being on her own after looking after two elderly people for many years and a sense of relief must have entered her thoughts.

Of course, the fact that Auntie Betty was very generous, and always gave us half a crown each time we visited her was not the only reason we went so often. She was highly entertaining. On this particular visit she had just acquired a television set. Most people had them by now, but the Aunties thought they wouldn't like it, it wouldn't be suitable for their delicate taste. But Betty was ready to give it a try.

She said, 'The things that I like most are the adverts.' Tom and me looked surprised. 'Except the hot chocolate one. I really don't like it – it sends me into a sort of trance.'

Thomas said, 'Why is this Auntie?'

And she said, 'Well, it goes hot chocolate, drinking chocolate, hot chocolate, drinking chocolate, ten times' by which time she was indeed going into a trance, sort of self-hypnosis, something which today would be considered quite the thing to do, a form of relaxation. Before her time, Auntie Betty was.

Anyway, eventually she regained her equilibrium and apologised for embarrassing us. We were delighted at the performance. Thomas advised her not to listen to that particular advert if it upset her. She was taken up with such mature advice from a young boy and said, 'Thank you, Thomas. How very clever of you, and so kind to think of me in that way. I think I have some money somewhere for you good, good boys.'

CHAPTER 28
RHEDA MANSION

Around about this time Thomas' family were moving house from Brookside to Rheda. They were leaving their little house on Trumpet Terrace to move into the West Lodge of Rheda Mansion, which was equally as small, but had potential to extend because it had a large piece of ground with it.

Thomas' family was growing in numbers and was soon to be four in total; Marta, Thomas, Peter and Marisha.

I was invited to tea for the first time soon after they settled in. I loved the Osowskis. They had a sort of Bohemian lifestyle. Thomas' dad, Felix, was from a completely different culture from ours. He looked foreign, with very thick black hair with a parting down the middle and quite long at the front. He was tall and slim and rather imposing. He looked like a Russian composer and spoke with a thick foreign accent. He was tactile with his children, often throwing them up in the air and squeezing them hard and muttering baby babble in Polish, but he stood no nonsense from them. He was quite strict when he had to be.

Mr Osowski always put me at my ease and talked to me in his broken English about school and working hard at my lessons. I liked him even though I found his loudness difficult at first. He was into the land so to speak. He had hens and ducks in his garden and a huge vegetable plot. He was almost self-sufficient in his agricultural ventures but I was of the impression he was dissatisfied with life in England. He had trained to be a welder and was forever piecing together old cars, making one good one from three old wrecks. He was a hard-working man.

Soon after their move to the West Lodge, Thomas told me they were emigrating to South Africa and as the process was taking some time they sold the Lodge and until they left for their new life in Cape Town, moved into Rheda Mansion as caretakers for the absentee landlord who owned it. This move proved to be of great interest to me because I was to be a frequent weekend visitor to their new temporary and very grand home.

Rheda Mansion was a huge Georgian mansion in its own grounds, complete with terraced lawns and broad sandstone staircases leading to what had once been a croquet lawn, but was now overgrown with long fine grass which resembled a miniature cornfield. The grounds were surrounded by exotic monkey puzzle trees, bamboos, strange conifers and rhododendrons.

It even had a summer house made of huge bamboo trunks with a thatched roof, hexagonal in shape and looked as though a strong gust of wind would render it flat to the forest floor in seconds. Its sheltered position in the small wood had saved it from two hundred years of high winds and so it was hanging on by a thread as indeed was the mansion itself.

The mansion had a glass tower to the west side with coloured glass built into the conical roof. From inside of the tower the red, blue and green glass shed a ghostly glow around the room and seemed to hold a thousand memories of previous occupants. It was said to be haunted.

The large entrance hall had a beautiful oak herringbone parquet floor leading to an impressive pitch-pine staircase with richly ornate balustrade and handrails. High up on two of the staircase walls were stags' heads complete with antlers, mounted on what looked like the family crest. The whole place was covered in cobwebs hanging like soiled lace curtains and smelt damp and cold. It was in a very neglected state, a bit like Miss Havisham's dining room in 'Great Expectations'.

The Osowskis occupied a south-facing apartment on the first floor that overlooked the lawns and the valley looking out to the sea beyond. It was faded grandeur on a large scale. The rooms were large and cold because of the floor to ceiling draughty sash windows, which rattled with the least sign of a breeze, but they were light and airy.

Thomas had discovered that if he opened the window leading onto a small balcony and left bread on it, a white barn owl would come every evening at dusk and feed for a few minutes, letting us have a perfect view of this spooky looking creature whose head seemed to swivel at 180° and whose green eyes penetrated the viewers on the other side of the glass.

The whole place was in a state of decay. The absentee landlord had an apartment on the ground floor consisting of several rooms which were always locked. Thomas and me were always trying to find the keys for these rooms but Antoinette had them safely hidden away.

After a short period of time Thomas's dad had decided to maximise on his assets and had put barrow-loads of deep litter on the parquet floor in the hall and had installed a dozen of so hens to occupy the otherwise unused space. He was a very resourceful man. This somehow didn't seem out of the ordinary to me although catching sight of the hens perched on the deer's antlers in the great hall when descending the stairs, sometimes gave me a bit of a fright.

The grounds had been laid out some 150 years earlier with walkways of fine gravel which had mossed over, but were still well defined and a circular walk from the mansion to the West Lodge took in woodlands and a small lake.

You could just imagine the ladies of the house chatting to each other and picking primroses from the edge of the paths as they took their constitutionals. My imagination ran riot. How sad it was to see it in such decline.

Talking of ladies, the new occupant, Thomas's Mam, Antoinette, was a real lady and so too were her sisters Betty and Clair who visited the Osowskis quite often. They were really of a past era and looked quite at home in their new surroundings. They were like the Brontë sisters. You could imagine them playing the harpsichord and writing their stories and brushing past each other in their wide frocks and lace caps.

Betty you know from my previous story of course, but Claire hasn't been mentioned before. She was a Headteacher at a large comprehensive school in Coventry. Head of the History department I believe, and she could give us all the relevant historical information on the mansion, and did so at length! She was a fascinating person.

Antoinette, however, was the practical one of the three. She had had to learn to be practical, bringing up her ever-growing family. In fact, while they were in the mansion the fifth member of the Osowski family arrived, Elizabeth, and the aunties were left in charge during Antoinette's confinement.

I imagine this must have caused problems for the aunties because they had no experience of looking after four young children, being maiden ladies and not too interested in the domestic side of life.

However, they gave it their best shot it has to be said, although Antoinette was very surprised to find there was still lots of food left in the house when she returned from hospital with her new daughter. Betty explained she'd fed the children mainly on breakfast cereal, as they all seemed to like it so much. Antoinette insisted they be put straight back onto solids before they all got rickets!

I can remember a parcel arriving one Saturday morning and Antoinette saying to Thomas, 'Oh, this parcel is from our Betty, I recognise her hand writing.' When she opened it, it was in fact from Betty and contained 2lbs of sausage and 1lb of bacon. It must have been in the post for a few days and it was as rotten as a pear and stank to high heaven. Antoinette had a few choice words to say about Betty, but conceded by saying, 'The thought was there, but can you believe she could think we would get the meat in any condition to eat? God love her.'

CHAPTER 29
THE HIDDEN DANGERS

We had been making a camp in the woods out of bamboo branches and some old Hessian sacks, when, out of the blue, came four policemen with their sniffer dogs. We thought they were after us for some reason although we couldn't imagine what we'd done wrong. The first policeman approached us shouting, 'We're looking for a little girl about ten years old. She has long brown hair and was wearing a light blue frock and a pink cardigan. Have you seen her anywhere today?' Tom and me just looked at each other in astonishment and both said together, 'No.'

The other policemen wandered off with the dogs pulling them along, but the first policeman walked towards us and restrained his dog with a muzzle. He looked in our camp and said, 'How long have you been here lads?'

I replied, 'We've had permission to play here.'

The policeman said, 'Don't worry, lads you're not in trouble. We're looking for a little lass who's gone missing and it's very important we find her. Are you sure you haven't seen a little lass wandering around by herself or maybe with a man?'

We both assured him we hadn't seen a single person all day and then he asked, 'Where do you live?' Thomas told him we lived in Rheda Mansion and he said, 'I think you should go home now lads, there's a big search going on and you'd be better out of the way.' So we turned on our heels and ran back to the mansion.

We passed another policeman with his dog in the woods and he shouted to us to get off home. By the time we got back to the mansion Antoinette was hurling the other kids back inside and looking very concerned.

Later, news filtered through that a little girl's body had been found in the lake next to the West Lodge. She came from Cleator Moor and Antoinette knew her family and was visibly shocked. She gave us all a lecture in her gentle but firm manner about the dangers of playing near the lake and told us never to go near it again.

I went back home on my bike later that afternoon and had to pass by the lake. Two policemen were guarding the entrance to the water and the gateway had been cordoned off with ropes. A small group of people had gathered and as I passed by I heard one of the policemen telling the people to go home. There was nothing anyone could do and they didn't want a big crowd to gather blocking the road.

I was sickened and didn't want to go anywhere near the lake ever again.

I only ever saw Antoinette dressed up in her Sunday best once. It was a warm Sunday afternoon and the whole family, myself included, was going for afternoon tea to the Seacote Hotel at St Bees. 'High Tea', Antoinette called it.

I was included because they were soon to be on their travels and Antoinette wanted me to come as a farewell treat. I'd never been to an hotel for 'High Tea' before and I thought it sounded rather grand. Marta, Thomas' older sister remarked on how lovely Antoinette looked and said she hadn't seen her in her beautiful dress before and Antoinette answered, 'No, I keep it only for state occasions and bonfire nights.'

My friends' days in England were numbered and I couldn't comprehend my loss when they finally departed. It was like a bereavement. I thought I would never see any of them ever again, but thankfully that wasn't to be the case. They returned to Cleator Moor two years later, minus Felix and that is a whole sad story in itself.

The mansion was demolished in the late 1950s and a local doctor bought the land and built what can only be described as a futuristic looking bungalow on the mansion site. It was all very '1960s' with angular rooms, a felt roof and floor to ceiling glass walls. It looked like a cross between a World War II bunker and a bus station. I don't know what the Georgian builders would have made of it.

CHAPTER 30
FISTICUFFS ON THE SLAG BANK

I was courting, of sorts, and my new girlfriend was Eleanor Drake. She had long jet-black straight hair with the face of an angel and the temper of a fish-wife. I like a girl with spirit. Our courtship was that of the early teenage type, with loads of pushing and strutting and mickey-taking. We met with a gang of friends and sort of wandered off around the slag bank, hand in hand, and stopped now and again after one of us pushed the other to the ground. Eleanor was a match for me in strength and a hell of a fighter. Somehow this excited me.

We used to snog a lot, with a bit of groping and wriggling about, not too intense. It was very clumsy and experimental. There were limits beyond which we never ventured, namely, below the belt; the middle section, although we would grind our groins together fully clothed and convince ourselves she'd get pregnant. It was all very frustrating, but irresistible at the same time.

On one of our trips to the slag bank somebody had brought a copy of 'Lady Chatterley's Lover' with them. It was actually only part of the book, probably only a dozen pages or so, and where they found them I'm not quite sure because the book was banned at the time but we were all going to have a read and see what all the fuss was about.

The slag bank dominated the view from the rear of Ennerdale Road and Birks Road and took the form of several small hills of chalky white and grey slag. It was an ugly legacy left behind by the nineteenth century industrialists, who mined the iron ore from dozens of pits around Cleator Moor and Whitehaven. They had their own foundry nearby and when they smelted the iron from the ore in the furnaces on Birks Road they dumped the molten slag and formed huge banks and mounds of the waste material, which looked like lava flows in some places.

There must have been tens of thousands of tons of the stuff dumped over a fifty year period or so. You can imagine the impact it had on the town. One of the necessary evils of its day, I suppose. It was the Aberfan of Cleator Moor, but fortunately the whole place was cleared years later, so no such disaster could occur. It was our very own adventure playground, complete with dark pools of clear water, full of newts and tadpoles and it looked like the surface of the moon or Grand Canyon, depending on the particular viewpoint from which you looked at it.

There wasn't a blade of grass that could grow on it. The only greenery was the odd wind bush, and a strange sort of mossy alpine type plant which had a lovely wee white flower on it in the Spring, and marguerites seemed to favour it. Apart from that it was sheer desolation. Some of this molten slag had obviously been poured when it was almost cold, and had formed itself into strange shapes, like the terracotta army in Beijing or the pyramids in Cairo. I loved it because it was so wild and haphazard, and it provided us with the perfect venue to indulge our carnal pleasures.

One of the party was reading excerpts from 'Lady Chatterley' in a little mossy hollow on the top of the slag bang and picking out the sexy bits, which were received with great enthusiasm by our little group. Although we all pretended to understand what they were doing, we really didn't have a clue. What was described in the book seemed impossible to me.

Raymond Graham and Eleanor and me were seeing who could throw the light lumps of slag the furthest and listening to the orator at the same time when the accident occurred. I thought Eleanor was on the ledge further down behind me when I turned round and threw this huge piece of black, round, heavy slag with all my might out towards the newt ponds. Unbeknownst to me, Eleanor had jumped up onto the ledge above where I thought she was and I let go of the piece of slag just as she appeared on eye level with me. She got the full force of the slag at point blank range in her face.

Silently, she went down like a ton of coal onto her knees. I thought I'd knocked her head off. The force of the impact was such, I'm sure you could have heard the bang as far away as the Market Square. We all panicked. Joan Farrer shouted, 'My God! Look what you've done to her!' Eleanor raised her head to look up at me and then closed her eyes and slumped over onto her face. A small cut above her eye was oozing blood and one side of her face was swollen like a balloon. I was sure I'd killed her.

Everybody was hopping round wondering what to do. Somebody shouted, 'She needs an ambulance!'

Somebody else said, 'She could be dead!' I was mortified. I climbed down from the ledge and she moved and raised herself up onto her knees.

I whispered, 'Are you alright, Eleanor?' And she bounced up and took a targe at me.

I shouted, 'I'm sorry, lass. I didn't see you. I thought you were below on the other ridge.'

She made a very swift recovery and planted a smack with her fist into my face. I lurched back to try to avoid her punch, but wasn't quick enough. She planted me one right between the eyes. I saw stars and felt the warm drip of blood on my top lip. I managed to restrain her and persuade her she would hurt herself even more if she didn't calm down.

I apologised for the accident and was full of remorse for the damage I had done to her, of which I eventually managed to convince her, with the help of the others. She refused to go to the hospital and have her injuries seen to, but instead insisted she'd be alright and just wanted to go home. She was a hard nut to crack, was our Eleanor. I had sustained a fat lip and a swollen nose, so we both sloped off home to lick our wounds and ponder on our misfortune.

The next day I met Eleanor on our way to school and we both erupted with laughter when we saw how we each looked. Her face was like a pound of raw liver. Her right eye was completely closed and both eyes were black and blue. My nose was spread across my face like a magic mushroom and my top lip was split.

We remained good friends for the duration of our school days and engaged in the odd bit of slap and tickle from time to time. She being a good Catholic lass, our encounters were more a bit of fun than high passion.

Of course, this sort of behaviour was in variance with our religious teaching and carried its fair share of Catholic guilt with it. It was hard to reconcile our natural urges with the very strict teaching of the Catholic church on the subject of sex, but nature will out.

Enjoy in haste and repent at leisure seemed to be the order of the day with me – and most of my contemporaries. We were taught to look upon such activities as dirty and unbecoming of good Catholic teenagers, but everything around us on the television and pictures was telling us the opposite. You had to strike a balance with your conscience and go regularly to confession.

I decided at this point in my life that I had to give up being an altar boy. I needed to be in a constant state of grace to receive the sacraments at Mass every day and I just wasn't. To cease being an altar boy wasn't a straightforward matter of just not turning up for Mass.

CHAPTER 31
MAKING A GOOD CONFESSION

I decided I'd make a good confession to Father McCann, the parish priest, and explain the situation of why I'd decided to give up being an altar boy. I've always found it better to be honest and straightforward with people and I needed to get it sorted out.

Father McCann was not totally sympathetic to my situation when I confronted him with my decision in confession. He insisted I should mend my ways and continue serving Mass. I had to have respect for myself and for the girls I was seeing, or, better still, not see these girls at all.

I wasn't backing down on this, and told Father McCann I would stop serving Mass for a period of time and reassess the situation when I'd had time to sort it out in my head. He tried to dissuade me, but finally conceded. I had to have a trial period away from Mass serving. I needed to come to confession every two weeks and pray for God's grace to help me keep pure.

During this trial period, I was kneeling in church one Sunday morning before ten o'clock Mass, not intending to go to communion, when Father McCann approached me and said, 'Sean, I need you to serve this Mass, I've got no altar server. Ian Paine hasn't turned in and Joe Udale is in bed sick.'

I said in a whisper, 'Father, I can't. I'm not in a state of grace.'

And he said, 'Come into the vestry with me and don't argue.'

I followed him into the vestry and he insisted on hearing my confession, which I made rather hurriedly. He gave me absolution and pointed at the cupboard where the cassocks were hanging and said, 'Now, get dressed. You've wasted enough of my time already.'

I served Mass that morning for the last time in my life. I decided, with much soul-searching, that I wasn't worthy of the honour of serving Mass, and I wasn't prepared to be compromised in this way ever again.

Father McCann never asked me again to serve Mass. I think he'd given me up as a lost cause. He still greeted me warmly and asked after my grandparents if he hadn't seen them for a while, but there was a distance between us which would never be breached.

CHAPTER 32
DAD'S REALLY BADLY

Dad's badly. He's on a diet of boiled fish, tripe cooked in milk and rice puddings. Not a bit of wonder he's badly, I thought. But, apparently a so-called bland diet is the only cure for a stomach ulcer, which is what Dad's got. When he's badly like this he rolls around on the living-room floor in agony. He gets really bad heads as well as the stomach pain and he's been taking a cocktail of aspirins, Beecham's powders and bicarbonate of soda, the Beecham's for the bad heads.

The house is like a twilight zone. All the curtains are drawn to keep the daylight out and Dad lies on the settee with a cold flannel on his head, like somebody not wise. Mam had to send for the doctor this time, and he says he needs bed rest for a week, to continue with the bland diet, but to gradually introduce some vegetables to help with the constipation. Dad says he's gone the whole hog, from shitting through the eye of a needle to popping bullets.

The doctor says the Beecham's and the aspirin have taken the lining off his stomach and aggravated the ulcers. He didn't mention the bicarbonate. Dad says he's got an arse like a blood orange. (He never loses his sense of humour.) The doctor has given him a prescription for a bottle to settle his stomach and some strong painkillers for the headaches. He's told him to lay off the aspirins especially, but dad says they're the only thing that can lift the bad heads, so what can you do?

As soon as the doctor went through the front door and Mam went back up to see Dad, he said, 'Bed rest, my arse. If he thinks I'm staying clocked in here for a week, he's got another think coming.'

Mam knew the seriousness of the situation and just exploded. 'You're doing exactly what the doctor says you're doing, Jay, if I've got to stitch you to the quilt. Now, do you hear me? Do you realise that ulcer could burst and you'd bleed to death before you got to the bottom of the ladder. Have a bit of sense, man, for the love of God.'

She was weeping by now and Dad knew he'd said enough. 'Well, you could be right, lass. But what are we going to do about money? There'll be none coming in with me lying in me bed.'

Mam just broke down and sobbed. 'Jay, lad, there'll be even less if you're lying in your grave. Now, listen. We'll be alright for money. I'll go and see Mammy if we have to and she'll see me alright. I don't want you to worry about money. I just want you to be well and back to normal, so do as the doctor says and stay in your bed.'

Dad was defeated. Bed rest it was to be, but he had a plan. 'Eileen,' he said when Mam went upstairs with some barley soup and dry bread.

Mam knew by his tone, even just one word was enough to put her on her guard. 'What, Jay,' she said. 'And no daft talk.'

'Well, lass, I've been thinking.'

'I was afraid you might have been,' she says.

'Well, lass, here am I, too badly to get out of me bed to clean me windows, but I could do a wee job from me bed, couldn't I? The doctor said bed rest. Well, what about if I made a few wreaths?'

Mam just looked at him and said, 'How are you going to do that from your bed?'

And Dad said, 'Well, it's just an idea, so hear me out.' Mam sat on the end of the bed and listened. She knew she'd had to let him have his say, no matter what.

So he explained he had a greenhouse full of pom-pom chrysanths, and Kinsella's in Whitehaven will take any amount of wreathes he has a notion to send them. If she picked the chrysanths, a dozen or so at a time, and he was sure there was a sackful of bracken from last Christmas, he could make the bases and dress the wreaths while he sat up in bed. Mam was speechless.

He said, 'There's only one thing. I'm going to need one of the lads to go down to Charlie Dorward's and bring some conifer clippings from the grotto. He's got loads lying round and he'll let me have a handful. What do you say?'

'What do I say? Do you really think I'm going to let you drag bracken and conifer clippings and rusty old wreath rings all round my good bed clothes? Do you think we're a load of bloody tinkers or something? You can forget about it, Jay.' And she stomped down the stairs and slammed the hall door.

When I got in from school Mam said, 'You'd better go upstairs with a cup of tea, Sean, for you father. He wants you to do a wee job for him.'

I said, 'How's he doing, Mam?'

And she said, 'He's not well, but he deserves to be not well because he won't give himself a chance, even when he's in bed. Now, go and see what he wants you to do.'

Dad was propped up on four or five pillows when I took his tea in the bedroom for him. He looked like Gandhi. I said, 'How's the fettle, Dad?'

And he said, 'I'm champion, lad, but your mother's got me stuck in this bloody bed like a prisoner, so I'm just humouring her for now, while it suits me. Now, here's what I want you to do. First, fetch me wreath shears and that sack of last year's bracken and me wreath rings, but before you do that, fetch the decorating sheets from off the loft and spread them on the bed and across the lino either side of the bed. I'm making a few wreaths to help me keep me sanity.

'Then I want you to go to the grotto and ask Charlie Dorward for some conifer clippings or a couple of branches, whichever he has handy. Get me the rings and bracken first, and when you've had your tea you can get me the conifer clippings from Charlie's, OK, lad? If you've any notion, you can give me a hand to make a few bases later on – if you've nowt else on, like.'

So I agreed to all dad's wishes. I felt he must be feeling better to be starting on the wreaths. Mind you, he didn't really look up to it to me. That night I heard him being sick in the bathroom. He used to stick his fingers down his throat and make himself sick, because he said it was the only way to ease the bad head. I can't settle when I hear him being sick, so I get my Huckleberry Finn out (the book, I mean) and read the dog-eared pages under the bedclothes with my flashlight, and now I'm drifting down the Mississippi with Tom Sawyer on a raft, dodging the sand banks, living off heron's eggs and wild rabbits, feeling the hot sun on my bare skin and drifting into a deeper sleep which will see me through until the morning and the beginning of another day at Seaview Place.

Before the end of Dad's confinement, which he cut short by three days, (because he said if he felt any better he couldn't stand it) there was a collection of big, plump, blowsy, white chrysanthemum wreaths, twenty-four in fact, with seven of them going to a neighbour's who had lost an elderly uncle, the rest to Whitehaven, where Mam says they'll be sold on for twice the price. The price, by the way, was twelve-and-six. Dad says if he could grow enough flowers and find a market for them, he'd give up the windows tomorrow. (Look out!)

I know I'm going to get a job when I leave school; of that I've no doubt, but what will I be doing in, say, ten years' time. I must admit I do wonder about the future with some concern. I want a job I can settle at; one that will give me satisfaction and a feeling of pride about what I'm doing. I couldn't stand to be always chopping and changing like Dad does.

Honestly, I could rhyme off at least a dozen jobs Dad's had in almost as many years. He just seems to lose interest after a while. He starts a job with great enthusiasm, telling Mam how marvellous this new job is. It can always knock the last job into a cocked hat. But the feeling never lasts very long and he becomes restless and ready for a change of scene. Thankfully, he always finds work. He has a motto he uses on these occasions: 'Never look back'. It's true, he never gives the past a second look. Maybe that's why he's always so happy. He lives for today.

I'm more like Mam, I think. I need to know what's ahead of me. I need to be working towards some future. Maybe because I've seen how Dad's attitude has had such a devastating effect on Mam, and giving her untold worries about bringing up the family, although I have to say Dad's never let us down. He's always worked and made good money, but I need more from my working life when the time comes, so I'm aiming for a good trade. Dad says a good tradesman can always find work.

CHAPTER 33
MARK ANTONY AND CLEOPATRA

Meanwhile back at St Cuthbert's we've got Miss Dempsey, Art and Craft, and Mr Holland, PE. The crack is, they're going out together. They're both newly qualified. She's a real doll; short skirts, skimpy tops, red nail varnish. She's drop-dead gorgeous and she knows it. We're doing the classical painters, Rembrandt and Michelangelo this week. There's none of the lads taking a bit of notice of what she's saying, we're just watching her stretch her arms up when she writes on the blackboard, revealing a tantalising silhouette of a pert pair of breasts and a glimpse of thigh. This is art. This is living art. Who needs boring old masters?

Last week we were doing pottery and Miss Dempsey gave us a real treat, unbeknownst to herself, I think, when she switched the potter's wheel on to show us how to mould a clay pot. The machine was sending vibrations up her arms and across her front. Honest to God, how she didn't spot us staring at her, I'll never know. It was like two pups trying to get out of a pillow-case. How I look forward to these double lessons on a Monday morning! It gives me the will to live after the weekend.

Anyhow, I think she's getting suspicious, because when last week's pottery lesson was finished and we were all exhausted watching her, she promised more of the same for this week's double lesson, but she's changed her mind on the pretext of having just done her nails. Mind you, they were pretty spectacularly crimson, but old masters, not pottery – it really isn't fair, is it?

Mr Holland (Jerry) looks like the all-American boy; tall, slim, dark and handsome, with his tight track-suit bottoms and his polo shirts. He's got the lasses foaming at the mouth. He passed by the maths room window, which is 2B form room, on the first floor looking down on the tennis courts, and Cecelia Keenan and Jacqueline Sharp wolf-whistled him out of the window. The next thing we knew, he burst into the classroom and demanded to know who had whistled at him. (Talk about God's gift to women! They could have been whistling at any of the fourth-year lads with him for all he knew.)

Anyhow, he was raging. Nobody would say who had whistled and so he threatened to go round the whole class, lads and lasses in turn with the cane until the culprit owned up. A short silence followed while he brandished the cane, which he took down from the blackboard. It had been placed there by Mr Singleton (Harry) the maths teacher for his convenience. Catherine Hughes was the first to snap. She said, 'I'm not getting caned for something I didn't do. It was Cecelia and Jacqueline, Sir.'

Well, if looks could kill! The two whistlers shot round and glared at Catherine, who was visibly shaken. I think she'd have been better off with the cane than what Cecelia and Jacqueline would do to her later. Mr Holland took the two girls to the front of the classroom and told them to go to Miss Cunningham after the lesson finished for the cane. The two girls took their punishment bravely and sat down at their desks.

As Mr Holland turned his back to leave, from out of the blue came a quiet wolf-whistle. It was Arthur McLaughlin. Mr Holland turned back like a flash and said, 'Who was that? I've had enough of you lot. You're all on detention tonight, so see how you all like that!' And left the room like a Russian ballet dancer.

CHAPTER 34
DOWN THE YELLOW BRICK ROAD

The reason we were unsupervised on this occasion was because Mr Singleton, who was also our RE teacher, was off sick and we were waiting for our relief teacher who was a little old lady called Mrs Armstrong. She'd been retired for some time, but came back now and again when one of our teachers was missing. The ironic thing was she wasn't a Catholic, and she was supposed to be taking us for RE. Honestly, we weren't a bad class. We were known to be one of the better classes, but she was giving us it on a plate.

'Now, class,' she started. 'I know this is supposed to be a religious lesson, and I'm sorry I'm a bit late. I had trouble finding you, but as I know very little about the Catholic religion, how about a game of bingo?' Well, we all just fell about laughing. The bloody woman was stark, staring mad! You know when everything feels just right for a bit of mischief? Well, this was one of those occasions. We were all in trouble anyway and we had detention after school. What did we have to lose? Might as well be hung for a sheep as a lamb. Here goes.

The poor old sod was totally oblivious to any of the hi-jinks which were being foisted on her. First of all, Martin Foley said, 'Miss, we usually start the lesson with a hymn and then a prayer,' to which she replied, 'Well, very, well, you start the hymn, lad. Go on, don't be shy.'

So Martin started to sing:

The Grand Old Duke of York
He had ten thousand men
He marched them up to the top of the hill
And he marched them down again.

Well, the rest of us were badly. We just howled. She reacted by saying, 'Now, class, I realise I should have been here at the beginning of the lesson to settle you down. I think maybe you're all a bit high spirited.'

This was superb. We'd never had one like this before. It just got better. Jacqueline Sharp remarked on how she liked her red shoes, and where did she get them from, she wouldn't mind a pair for herself. The poor old lass thought she was being serious and told her how she'd had them for years, couldn't just remember where she'd bought them, but thanked her for her kind remark.

Then Cecelia Keenan remarked on how gorgeous her hair was and would she mind letting her back-comb it a bit to give it some height. To which she agreed. Cecelia back-combed her hair into great knots and tatters, till she looked as if she had mange, and all the while the lasses were telling her how gorgeous it looked. She was delighted with the attention.

Meanwhile, one by one we were leaving the classroom, until only about three or four of the more serious classmates were left when the bell went. She was heard to have said on leaving the classroom how few children she had in the class. She was sure there were more when she arrived.

As she disappeared into the corridor, looking like Dorothy in the Wizard of Oz, with her red shoes going down the yellow brick road to the emerald city somewhere over the rainbow, back to cloud cuckoo land where she belonged, God love her. I felt really horrible for the way we treated her, but she seemed none the worse for the experience.

CHAPTER 35
DAD'S LITTLE FOIBLES

Dad had a few habits that really annoyed Mam. For a start, he sometimes poured his tea out of his cup into the saucer to drink it. He'd do it regularly if Mam didn't pull him up about it. She'd say. 'That's a terrible habit, Jay, I don't know how you've been brought up.'

And he'd say, 'Well, lass, I wasn't born with a silver spoon in my mouth like you were.'

And she'd say, 'No, you were born with a wooden clog in your mouth, by the table manners you display.'

Dad loved this banter and wound Mam up with ease. She didn't have his sense of humour. He thought nothing of farting at the table, always excusing himself, mind you. Mam would always be outraged at this and go and fling a window open, shooting him the most dirty look. And he'd say, 'I don't know what you're fussing about, Eileen, there's no smell of them.

Well, she'd rise to the bait every time. 'No smell,' she'd say. 'There wouldn't be, would there? It's only gas coming straight from your bowel, why would it smell? I'm sure the Guinness book of records would be interested to hear about the only man in the world whose pumps had no smell.' You see, she couldn't make herself use the word 'fart'; it was too coarse a word for her. It was always a 'pump'.

Dad loved to wind her up like this. He'd carry on, 'Oh, and you don't pump, Eileen, do you? Except for that Christmas afternoon, lass. But I'll let you off with that one; after all, the food was very rich.'

'You have to bring that one up, don't you?' Mam said. 'The only time I slipped up in public.' By this time Mam had begun to see the funny side of the conversation, but wanted it to stop because she was embarrassed about her indiscretion.

It was after we'd all settled down to watch a Bing Crosby Christmas special on the telly. Mam and Margaret had just finished washing the pots from the Christmas day tea and we were all seated except Mam, who finally put her pinny away and joined us on the settee. She bent over to tidy the coffee table before she sat down and scopped one up. It was only a double-barrelled tight one. I think it got trapped in her corselet by the sound of it.

Dad was like a dog with two tails. He shouted out, 'Go on, Eileen, lass! Let them rip!' Poor Mam. She blushed like a maiden aunt.

He said, 'That's better out than in, lass. Now, let me get you a wee glass of sherry, or would you like a port to settle your digestion?'

'Alright, Jay, you've had your joke. Now, let's just drop it,' says Mam, still not quite believing she'd been caught short.

He went on, 'Are you sure you're alright, lass? That sounded a bit wet, you know,' laughing hysterically.

Mam wasn't used to being the butt of the joke and shot him a look. 'That's enough, Jay,' she said.

Dad said, 'You're dead right that's enough, lass. We don't need the bloody Bing Crosby show in here tonight, lass, we've got pump competitions going on, and I'm the next contender very shortly.' Mam just ignored him this time; she knew that with the least bit of encouragement he'd keep it up all night.

The other habit Dad had which annoyed Mam was the evacuation of his false teeth at the table during a meal. Dad would spit them out into his hands and lick the crumbs off from round the gums. Mam would throw a complete wobbler when he did that. She'd say, 'For God's sake, Jay, it's like having a meal with a pig eating with you. Nobody wants to see your teeth when they're eating.

'Well, the trouble is, lass I get bits stuck under the plate and it annoys me.'

'Yes, well, it's because they don't fit properly, Jay. You need new ones, for god's sake. You've had them since Adam was a lad.'

'Aye, and I'm keeping them, because I have no intention of breaking a new pair in, so you'll just have to put up with it, Eileen.'

'Well, at least go to the sink and rinse them under the tap. It makes me feel sick watching you spit them out.'

Dad's chin seems to double in size when he has no teeth in, and his face sinks right in. If I had false teeth I wouldn't be seen dead without them. When he puts them back in and starts talking he sounds as if he's got a pair of castanets in his mouth, he's really funny.

CHAPTER 36
FLICKA, THE OLD SLAPPER

We've had Flicka for nearly two years now, and she's an absolute peach. She's a 'people dog'. She loves the company of people. She wanders from one to another of us, seeking attention the whole time, and she gets it, but she's broken down at the moment and has to be watched like a hawk in case she slopes off.

Every morning there's a heap of lovelorn dogs at our back door, waiting with bated breath for a glimpse of their heroine. They can jump the garden gate and fence, so we can't even leave Flicka tied up in the garden. This means more regular walks on the lead, which is a pain because she's not really used to a lead.

She's usually very obedient and sticks close by when we're out walking, but when she's broken down, she's pulling the arms off us to get free. So, against every instruction and threat of a murdering from Mam, I let her off the lead on the Big Hill.

Well, there wasn't a dog in sight, and Flicka had nearly pulled my arm out of its socket. She shot off like a thing possessed, straight across St Cuthbert's school field and into the arms of a lurcher you could have had a ride on. It was as big as a donkey. I shot off after her, but by the time I'd gone hoarse from shouting her back and had a stitch from chasing after her it was too late.

She was totally shameless. As soon as I got within ten yards of them they stopped and moved off up the field to a safer distance and then started again. This went on for at least half an hour, and I was exhausted running after them, never mind them. At one point I managed to catch hold of Flicka's collar and tried to pull her away. The big lurcher panicked and somehow twisted himself round, facing away from her.

It was hideous. They were stuck together, facing opposite ways, like Siamese twins. I'd seen this happen before from the geography room window, and Mr Hennedy, the caretaker had to throw a bucket of water over them to separate them. It wasn't Flicka that time, mind you. But where the hell am I going to find a bucket of water from in the middle of the playing field?

It really looked as if their bums were grafted together. I thought we'd need to get a vet to separate them. Every time I attempted to approach within a couple of yards of them they both started to bare their teeth and growl. It was horrible. I couldn't believe it was our Flicka. She was like a different dog. Flicka eventually started to whimper and I knew I had to do something soon or she could be in a lot of trouble.

I reckoned the bucket of water must have given the two dogs a fright and that caused them to separate, so I devised a cunning plan. I thought if I take some steps away from the dogs, and suddenly start to charge at them, screaming at the top of my voice, they'd be terrified and pull apart.

I went in at them like General Custer at the Battle of Little Big Horn, and to my surprise they just walked away from each other without even a backward glance. I ask you! Talk about slam bang, thank you, ma'am! Well, I suppose they know no better, they're not exactly looking for a relationship. Flicka stank like an old kipper box and was wet from head to foot. If she isn't in pup after this lot, I'll eat hay with a horse.

Of course, I didn't need to eat the hay. Nine weeks later Old Slapper produced the loveliest litter of eight brown and black pups you ever saw. Four she was allowed to keep, four went into the bucket. She gave birth at nine o'clock on Saturday morning. It was like shelling peas. Not a cuck out of her.

She watched while Dad popped the last four pups into the bucket of water beside her and didn't even get up to look for them. She was the worst mother in the world to those pups. We had to hold her down, five to six times a day so the pups could feed from her. She couldn't have cared less about them.

Our cousin, Diane, was given the pick of the litter and she chose the liveliest pup, which she called Kim, and he went to live next door with her and Aunty Lily, who spoiled him rotten to his dying day. He was a belter of a dog. The others went to neighbours and Flicka never acknowledges a single one of them from the day they were weaned. Aren't dogs funny?

CHAPTER 37
THE LINE AROUND
THE BEDROOM CEILING

I love to lie awake in bed and listen to the quietness of the day beginning. Beginning for me, that is, because I can hear the gentle chink of milk bottles being carefully placed on all the front steps on Seaview Place. I can hear the quiet response to the milkman from some neighbour's dog. I can hear the melancholy refrain of the banty cocks drifting over from Abe Woodburn's farmyard and Mrs. Salmon next door emptying the ashes from the coal fire into the ash bin.

I hear all these things, yet it feels quiet. There are no traffic sounds, so every little blip of noise from outside is audible. It's life's little rituals, which seem to happen automatically.

I'm not part of these work-a-day rituals yet, I'm still in the glorious state of childhood. I can enjoy the luxury of observing things being done all round me and having the responsibility for none of it. I lie in quiet reverie and complete happiness.

Our music teacher, Ma Murphy, played us some music last week called 'Peter and the Wolf' by somebody called Prokofiev. She also played us 'The Sorcerer's Apprentice', and she tells us the story the music was supposed to be telling, but I reckon that's all bollocks. The music didn't mean anything to me. It was just a load of noise; loud and soft jarring sounds. There are some clever people in the world, who can make sense of so much, and here am I, happy to be warm and comfortable, staring up at the ceiling, hearing Stephen gently breathing next to me in the double bed.

I follow the line between the wall and ceiling all the way round the room with my eyes. I know it so well. The bit where Dad cut the paper slightly short and pieced a bit in, just above the dressing table. It was a good match, but I know it's there. There's a crucifix on the wall directly above the light switch as you come through the door. The nail is bang in the middle of the wallpaper joint and you can follow the line back up to the ceiling.

The ceiling is brilliant white and the wallpaper is mauve and peppermint green stripes. Mam doesn't like it now it's on. She liked it on the roll in the shop, but admitted she chose it in a hurry and went for a stripe because Dad told her not to get a paper with a match because it takes longer to put on. I think it's beautiful. It makes a statement. You have to confront it as soon as you waken up. It's not one of those poncy flowery papers. Mind you, the sacred heart picture next to the wardrobe looks a bit scary with it.

We used to have the sacred heart picture in the living room at Cleator, but since we moved to Seaview Place it's been housed in our bedroom. It has a red light behind the heart and when you plug it in the heart lights up, but the flex won't reach the plug from where it is now, thank God. We've got a great big pot statue of Our Lady of Lourdes, and a little plastic statue of St Martin on the dressing table. Honestly, you can practically do the Stations of the Cross without getting out of bed. It's a bit too much.

I gave Dad a hand to paper the bedroom. I pasted the paper for him while he had a fag. The secret, he says, is getting the first length on plumb. The rest is plain sailing after that. Dad sized the walls first; well, one wall where he was going to start. I sized the rest. He played around with the first length and used a spoon on a piece of string for a plumb bob, satisfying himself it was plumb, and then cut ten lengths of paper all the same length for me to paste. He showed me how to fold the paper and lay it over the back of a chair to soak, keeping all the edges covered.

When I get to the line above the wardrobe I smile to myself, because I know what lies beneath the perfectly straight line of mauve and green paper. Behind the wardrobe is a patchwork of short off-cuts pieced together; ends of rolls. If Dad can avoid breaking into the last roll of wallpaper, he'll do it, supposing he has to leave a piece off behind the curtains, which he's been know to have done before. It's a principle, you see.

He loves to take the unopened roll, place it in Mam's hands and say, 'Take this back to Athy Pearson and get a refund, lass. I made do without it.' Mam would just put her eyes up to the ceiling and say, 'I hope you haven't missed a wall out, Jay. There's no point in having a full roll left if the job's only half done, you know.'

This argy-bargy would continued until Mam had inspected the work and decided a blind man on a galloping horse would never notice it and gave her seal of approval. So I had an affinity with this room. It felt right. It didn't jar (except for the sacred heart picture, and the dodgy pieced bit above the dressing table). It felt like a good place to be, and I could drift off into the land of nod for a brief half hour before Mam called us up for school.

Talking of school, Ma Murphy, our music teacher, the one of 'Peter and the Wolf' fame, had a much more agreeable lesson prepared for our next double music lesson. She told us she intended to let us take part in an experiment; a musical experiment. She maintained that the classics would last forever and the pop music of the day would be forgotten by us, even before we left school in three years' time.

So, to make this an official experiment, she asked us to debate among ourselves for a half hour or so, each one of us writing down our two favourite current pop songs, then find the most popular two songs, and next week if someone would like to bring the records into class she'd play them. She would then put the results of the survey into an envelope, and on our very last music lesson, before we leave school she'd open the envelope and see how many of us could remember the names of the songs. She even suggested that she could guarantee some of us won't even remember the songs at all. We didn't believe her, of course, but it was better than Brahms and Liszt any day of the week.

Ma Murphy was a really nice lady, she didn't need to shout and threaten people in the classroom. She had a way with her, and most of us responded to that. She once brought a cine film of her and her family on holiday in Spain into the classroom. She'd set the projector and screen up and regaled us with shots of her in a swimsuit frolicking in the blue waters of the Mediterranean and playing with a beach ball with her daughter and son on the golden sands. I was mesmerised and thought how I'd love to swim in the warm waters of the Mediterranean, but it's not something I thought I'd ever be likely to do. Blackpool was the nearest thing to warm blue waters I was ever likely to get.

The two most popular songs of that week in September 1961 were *My Boy Lollipop* by Millie and *Going to the Chapel* by the Dixicups and, true to her word, on our last lesson with Ma Murphy in March 1964 she produced the envelope which we'd all completely forgotten about from her desk drawer. She held it up and asked if anyone could tell her what was in the envelope. Nobody could, so she gave us a clue by producing two forty-five records in their rather grubby sleeves and went to the record player and started to play the first record. It was *My Boy Lollipop*. And when that was finished she played the other, which was of course *Going to the Chapel*.

We all remembered *My Boy Lollipop*, but couldn't remember which was the second record we'd elected to be our favourite of 1962. This served to prove her point that pop music is very transient and classical music would last forever. She went on to play a short excerpt from 'Peter and the Wolf' and saw the expressions of recognition from her attentive class and finished off her lesson by telling us there was a wonderful world of adventure and excitement awaiting us, and to go out and embrace it with open arms, and encouraged us to listen to all kinds of music because it was life-enhancing and uplifting.

She finally said, 'Good luck, class and God bless.' I'll always remember her sincerity and kindness. Ma Murphy was spot on.

CHAPTER 38
THE COOPER-HOLMES'S

We met the Cooper-Holmes lads on the old disused railway line near No. 2 Hollow (a bottomless pond, part of the old Crowgarth mines), which was a favourite haunt of Stephen's and mine. Their names were John, the elder of the two, and David. They lived in the police houses on Crag Road; their Dad was a Bobby. They were about our age, give or take a year or so, and they arrived in their rather splendid bogey.

Bogey season was here, which was late September and early October, after the summer holidays and before the dark nights, a hectic two months of creativity. The bogeys were home-made contraptions and very individual in design. Theirs had something we'd never seen before; it had only three wheels, two at the back and a single front wheel, pivoted to guide it by.

We engaged in conversation about the unusual bogey and they suggested we swap and go down the line to Moor Row on them. We were well impressed with their three-wheeler and recognised its superior engineering qualities. Mind you, it couldn't take the rough treatment our less elegant, four-wheeler one could, but it was a talking point and broke the ice nicely for us.

We became very good friends, camping out in their green Icelandic mountain tent in their big back garden and going for bike rides to Ennerdale and St. Bees. We whiled away much of our home time together. Unfortunately, shortly after we became acquainted the Cooper-Holmes's acquired a nightly paper round, which meant we didn't see much of them on week nights.

After a couple of months of doing the round, David came round to our house to ask if Stephen and me fancied starting a new round between us, as his boss was trying to recruit new lads to expand the coverage of the paper, the Barrow Mail. We jumped at the chance, and, after discussing with Mam, assuring her the round would only take an hour every weekday night and two hours on Saturday because there was the pink sports paper as well as the ordinary Barrow Mail on Saturdays, she agreed.

This enterprise would prove to be a nice little earner. We had an interview on the market square, where the papers were delivered every night. The paper boss, Ken, was a little pink-faced ginger-haired bloke with orange teeth, who had bad breath and an attitude problem. He weighed us up, looking at us as if he had a piece of shit on his nose-end. David had warned us; he said he was a shifty little turd, but as long as we were on time and got the money in, he's OK. He said, 'Mind, I want no pissing about if I give you a start. I know what it's like when a bunch of lads get together. You find your own customers, don't steal anybody else's and keep regular or you won't keep your customers.'

Stephen and me just kept nodding in response, not knowing quite what to make of him. He said he'd leave us with a dozen papers on Monday night to see how we got on and any we didn't sell we'd have to return or we'd be charged for them. That sounded fair enough. We already had seven customers on our own avenue because we'd gone door-knocking the night before. Stephen told him this but he didn't seem impressed. He said, 'Finding them is the easy bit. Keeping them is what's important.' Then he turned his back, climbed into his white van and disappeared into the night without a 'ta-ta' or a 'kiss-my-arse'.

The Holmes's were laughing their socks of and came running over to hear how we'd got on. I said, 'Alright, I think. He's letting us have a dozen papers on Monday night to see how we get on, but what a horrible bloke he is, isn't he, David?'

'I told you he was a little turd, didn't I? But you don't have to bother about him – just take your papers and say nothing.' The Holmes's had just over forty regular customers they delivered to and the odd sales on the square when the papers arrived. There was a wealth of untapped punters just waiting for our knock.

And so it proved to be. Within a month we had over sixty regulars and we broke new ground by going into the pubs with any spare papers we had left over, usually round about a dozen or so, varying every night. Suddenly, Greasy Ken, the boss, was all over us like a rash, congratulating us and generally kissing our arses. We just kept requesting more papers and returned the 'shit on the end of the nose' expression he first greeted us with.

The price of the papers was four pence to the customer and we got a shilling for every ten papers sold, so we were making nearly seven shillings a night. Multiply that by six and add the forty-odd pink sport papers on Saturday night, which we sold mostly in the pubs, we were raking in well over four pounds a week, sometimes over five pounds between the two of us. We were millionaires.

Mam wouldn't let us keep all the money. She insisted on taking four pounds and putting it into the post office for us. Anything over four pounds we could keep. That was a bit hard to take, but we decided we'd save the money for a new rally bike apiece. We'd seen them in Mark Taylor's in Whitehaven. They were £49.19s.6d, but at this rate we could afford them if we saved for just over six months. We would still be well off, with three or four bob a week in our pockets.

One of our best pubs was Pat McGrath's on Aldby Street. It was always chocker with hound dog men and pigeon men. It was due to be demolished soon, along with the rest of Aldby Street, North Street and some of Birks Road and all of Fletcher Street.

These clusters of houses were built, along with most of Cleator Moor, to house the mine and foundry workers who arrived nearly a hundred years ago from Ireland and many parts of England, Scotland and Wales. They had been built in a hurry and were very small and close together. They had only a narrow back yard and no gardens. Many of the houses still had gas lighting and poor sanitation, so people were being moved out onto new estates like ours on Priory Drive and Melbreak Avenue.

Pat McGrath's was the last property to be vacated. It looked like the Last Chance Saloon at the end of the street, surrounded by abandoned houses, some with windows broken and curtains billowing in the wind, obviously not wanted by the departed tenants and all it needed was a cartload of tumbleweed released at the bottom of the street and it could be used as a set for 'High Noon'.

The pub itself had no paint on the doors and windows and bare floorboards throughout. Its walls were stained a deep sepia colour from a million cigarettes and pipes. The bar was beer-stained and had the original spittoons still in place around its perimeter. I never saw any sawdust in it, but occasionally a splodge of spit, partly dried up, could be seen shining on the grey slate receptacle. The purveyor of the misplaced poik must have forgotten himself for a moment and slipped back to some time not so long past when chewing tobacco was popular with the miners and every bar had a spittoon.

You see, they could chew tobacco down the pits where they couldn't smoke, for obvious reasons, so many of them got their daily fix of nicotine by chewing and giving up the smoking habit altogether. Some of them in Pat's still chewed tobacco and spat the brown deposits into the fire. It looked as if it had been attacked by a muck-spreader, all the off-target tobacco spit burned on by the heat of a constant fire.

It smelt of foist, stale beer, tobacco and old men's clothes, but by God, they all knew how to buy newspapers. Our best Saturday night's sale of the wee pink paper was Derby Day, 1962. We sold forty-three papers in Pat McGrath's alone and had to phone Greasy Ken for extra copies.

I remember one Saturday night when I was collecting my paper money from the Victoria on Ennerdale Road, I'd noticed a lady seated on her own in the snug. She was all dressed up to the nines, blonde bouffant hair, bright red lips and a very revealing neckline under her ocelot fur coat. She looked like a ship's figurehead with breasts to match. She was a well-known lady of the night by the name of Bridey. She was either waiting for a customer or had been stood up by one. I felt sorry for her.

She didn't seem to notice me. She just stared straight ahead, looking at a blank wall. Suddenly I noticed a trickle of water coming from under her and making its way to the end of the bench, where it formed a small puddle. She just kept looking straight ahead as if she hadn't noticed. Just then the landlord, looking through the hatch in the wall, noticed the pool of water. He charged round to where she was sitting and pulled her up by her arms and said, 'Get your dirty self out of here and piss somewhere else!'

Years later the same lady was seen throwing her dog into Whitehaven docks by a man who was walking his own dog. He was so incensed by what he saw, he got hold of her and threw her in after it. The tide was partly out and poor Bridey had to plough her way back to dry land through yards of slime and mud, looking like something from Quatermass and the Pit. How weird is that?

Talking about Fletcher Street.... was I talking about Fletcher Street? Well, anyhow, I had seven customers on Fletcher Street and on Friday, when I collected my paper money I used to dread one of my Fletcher Street customers opening their door because the smell would have knocked you on your back. No kidding! What the hell they must do in their house to kick up such a stink God only knows.

CHAPTER 39
YOU CAN SEE IT, SMELL IT
AND TASTE IT

Have you ever smelt a dirty house? It's hard to explain. Can you imagine baby's sick mixed with a bad case of underarm odour? Well, you're somewhere near if you can. The door opens and instantly you're enveloped in this warm, slimy, greasy stench. It's like a genie exploding out of a lamp straight up your nose.

The slow movement of the door being opened (because these smelly people never do anything fast) allows you to observe the dog turd behind the door being spread over the doormat like a Dairylea triangle, releasing its pungent, but recognisable smell to mingle with the unrecognisable other smells.

The concrete skirting board, last painted lavatorial green in 1927, pitted with soil, ash and snail trails, and the bamboo-patterned, once light green and cream wallpaper, turned a musty khaki and orange, ripped off half way up the wall to reveal a patch of soiled mud-coloured bare plaster.... that's just first impressions.

Then there's the delay (because these same people never expect you, even though I've collected every Friday for nearly a year) because they can't find any money. So you get treated to a view of the big picture; straight down the lobby into the hell-hole they call a kitchen. It's more like a byre than a kitchen. The obligatory clothes pulley with dirty/clean washing hanging over the fireplace, trapping Mrs Cockbain with its damp, slimy, corduroy tentacles. She ratches along the mantelpiece, knocking over a plate of tomato soup, left there from last Monday's tea, onto the dog, which doesn't even get up. It just bends its head round and licks the semi-congealed plop off its back.

By now I'm nearly baulking my puddings up. She still hasn't found her purse. Holding my breath and turning round to face the road now and then for a quick intake of breath, I feel the warm damp odour clinging to the exposed skin on the back of my neck. I subconsciously lift my arm up to have a quick sniff to make sure it's not me, satisfying myself I'm clean. I must be clean, because I've discovered our Margaret's 'Mum' roll-on underarm deodorant in the bathroom cupboard and I'm using it religiously every day, even if I don't wash under my arms. I'm even wearing our Barry's 'Jet' aftershave. Dad says I smell like a tart's handbag.

Just before I throw up the entire contents of my stomach, she hobbles up the hall like Quasimodo's mother, her pinny stained with at least a month's worth of spilt meals and a mild haemorrhage. She hands me a very grimy pound note. My God! I'm going to have to hold my breath and count out her change into her hand at the same time. You know, she never utters one single word, that woman, but by God, you never forget her. She leaves her mark on your nostrils for hours after she closes the door, containing the smell from hell, ready to unleash it onto the next unsuspecting visitor.

Fletcher Street must rank as one of the worst streets for me on my paper round, because I had probably the worst experience of my entire paper boy career there. One wet November Friday night, tired and soaked to the pelt after completing my round and a good half hour in the pubs cut short because I was uncomfortably wet, I knocked on the door expecting payment for the week's papers. I could see a light shining under the parlour door from the front window of the house, and was surprised that I was getting no response from my knocking.

I continued to knock for a few minutes longer and then noticed lights suddenly appearing under the front door. I knocked again with no response. I thought I must have not noticed the lights from under the front door when I first started to knock, because there was no sign of anybody inside. I decided to push the paper through the letter box and call on Saturday for my money.

Just as I pushed my face forward to find the letter box in the dark as I was on level with it, the letter box opened and a shaft of light shot onto my face. I was surprised and rather shocked by this sudden streak of light and momentarily blinded by it. Before I could pull my face away to poke the paper through I heard someone behind the door do what I thought sounded like clearing their throat.

The next thing I knew, my face was completely covered in spit. Great globs of thick phlegm. It was in my ears and in my hair and even in my open mouth. I was totally sickened. I rushed over to the gutter and splashed rain water over my face and hair and even rinsed my mouth out with it. Who the hell could be responsible for such a filthy trick?

I was so shocked I did something completely out of character and kicked the door several times, almost breaking it down. I opened the letter box and screamed for someone to open the door. By this time the hall was in darkness and the streak of light streaming from under the parlour door was gone. No-one would respond to my calls. My final gesture was to open the letter box and shout at the top of my voice through it, 'You dirty filthy bastard!' I was never ever any wiser as to who had spat at me or why.

The following morning I went back to the owner of the house, who was horrified by my tale and said she was away on Friday at her sister's at Frizington and hadn't got back until quite late. As far as she was aware nobody should have been in her house and nobody to her knowledge had a key. She paid me my money and asked me if I would tell the police about what had happened, because she was concerned as to how somebody had gained access to her house to do such a horrible thing. This I did, and went with her to the police station and told the police who in my opinion, maybe to give the lady some peace of mind, implied that maybe I'd got the house mixed up in the dark. I knew I hadn't. I recognised the letter box. (You do after a while.) To this day it remains a mystery.

Fletcher Street has certainly hit the news again this week, because the crack's going round that there's a lass who goes to Ehenside School from Fletcher Street was sent home last Friday after a visit from the nit nurse. She kept her hair in a great big beehive, about two feet from the top of her head. She looked like one of those women from the court of Louis XV1. She just needed to powder it and give herself a beauty spot. The nit nurse was surprised to have found mice in it. Now, can you believe that? What kind of a comb would you use to get rid of mice? (You wouldn't need a fine-tooth comb, that's for sure.) I bet the nit nurse nearly had kittens. Actually, that would have been quite handy – they could have caught the mice. Alright, I'm only joking.

We kept the paper round going for nearly two years, until we both started work, and our cousin Raymond took it over for a while, picking out the best of the round for his convenience, and what happened to it after that I haven't a clue. Isn't it strange how something so important and totally all-consuming can be replaced with a single turn of events in our lives? We move on without a backward glance, it seems. Stephen and me enjoyed a year or so more of horse play and fisticuffs with the slightly mad David and more sedate John Cooper-Holmes until they eventually moved to Distington, where Mr Holmes had been promoted to village Bobby, complete with his own police station and house attached. We all went our own separate ways after that and lost contact.

CHAPTER 40
TOO MUCH INFORMATION

I've just discovered Parma Violets. My favourite sweet to date was Midget Gems, but they've been superseded by the beautifully scented, mauve coloured Parma Violets. I could eat them all day without a rest. I'm telling you that because I'm sucking a couple while I'm waiting for my turn to see Dr Smith about the slightly delicate problem I have in the nether regions. Mind you, my problem isn't half as bad as one of the old ladies who are exchanging complaints with a vengeance.

The first lady, I'll call her Maggie (that isn't her real name) is telling Grace (not her real name) that she thought it was piles so she'd been using Vaseline. Grace tuts sympathetically and Maggie goes on to explain it was getting worse, so she'd been to see Dr Smith last week and he said it was kins.

Grace says, 'What kind of kins, Maggie?'

'Well, lass, just like when you get splits in your finger joints and they won't heal. You know what I mean, Grace.'

Grace nods and their heads move nearer together to keep the crack private, but Grace is deaf so Maggie continues in a loud whisper, loud enough to be heard outside on Kiln Brow. That's where Dr Smith's surgery is; it's in Mrs Davis's front two rooms. I think she must live in the back of the house and let Dr Smith use the front.

The waiting room is very old-fashioned; it's got chairs all round the room. Not a one matches. There's a black leatherette one with big carved back and legs; some of the horse hair is poking out of a split in the corner of the cushion. And there's a rocking chair that's seen better days in the far corner. Children aren't allowed to sit on a chair if an adult comes in and there's no chairs left. I don't even attempt to sit, because I'll no sooner get seated than some old codger will fall through the door and I'll be obliged to give it up, so it's easier to just lean against the wall and hope Dr Smith doesn't have to spend a lot of time with each patient.

There's seven before me. My problem could well have cured itself before I'm seen. There's two rather stout middle-aged ladies sitting either side of the door and being constantly interrupted from their small talk by the door opening and closing. The one in the hat that looks like a dead hen is busy telling the other how great their new-fashioned coats are. She says, 'You can just slip them on over your pinny; nobody would know.'

The other lady with the fat red face and floral headscarf and looks as if she's going to burst, agrees. She says 'Aye, they're great, Agnes. Nice and loose-fitting, lass. No tight buttons and belts, they're far better.'

No tight button and belts! She's the full of that coat, even though it's supposed to be loose-fitting. She'd never get a belt round her if she tried. She's busy telling dead-hen-hat lady how she's only here for a note from the doctor to take to the dentist for her to have her teeth out. No kidding, she's got a smile like a ripped wellie.

Anyhow, back to the bit of crack between Maggie and Grace (which are not their real names). There seems some confusion. Grace says, 'Where exactly have you got the kins, Maggie?'

Maggie hesitated before answering and looked round at the rest of the patients, who are just as eager to find out, and whispers something that sounds like 'Up me....' And something I can't quite hear.

Nor can Grace. She says,' Where, Maggie?'

And Grace says, loud enough for all of us to hear, 'Up me back passage.' Well, everybody in the room shifted about and gave the odd embarrassed cough, hoping that that's the end of it. Not a hope.

Grace says, 'Oh, Maggie, I've never heard of that before. What's the cure?'

'Well, that's the trouble,' says Maggie. 'If this ointment doesn't do the trick, I'll have to have the operation.' (Slight pause.)

'Which operation is that, then,' says Grace.

'Well,' says Maggie as she darts round the waiting room with her eyes. 'They'll have to stretch it.'

Grace says, 'Stretch what, lass?'

Again, Maggie scans the room and decides to go for it. 'Me bloody arse, Grace, what do you think?'

Poor Grace nearly passed out on hearing this gruesome information, along with everybody else in the room. 'Oh, lass, they'll surely chloroform you for that, won't they?'

'Aye, by God, they will,' says Maggie. 'There's no way I'm having that done while I'm conscious.' She goes on, 'You see, they have to shove....' And before she has chance to finish her sentence a lady sitting opposite them blurts out, 'For God's sake, Maggie, spare us all the gory details, will you, I've just had me breakfast.'

Maggie says, 'Aye, well, you shouldn't be listening to other people's private conversations, Mary Ellen, and you wouldn't be offended.'

The other lady says, 'Listening to other people's private conversations! I'd have to be stone deaf not to hear the pair of yers.'

I thought they were going to get to blows, when Mrs Davis comes in with a shovel of coal and gives the women a look that would have stopped the clock. She says, 'Can we have some quiet in here, please? The doctor has a patient in with him and he needs peace and quiet to see properly to his patients, as I'm sure you will all realise.' Well, from there on you could have heard a pin drop, which was a shame, really, because I'm never going to find out what needed to be shoved where and why.

There's no proper system in Dr Smith's surgery. You just take a seat (or not) and wait your turn. Now, I'm so absorbed in the kins crack (excuse the pun) that I haven't really noticed who came in immediately after me. The trick is you have to memorise all the faces of the people who are already in the room when you arrive, and as soon as the last person who was in the room when you arrived has seen the doctor, it's your turn. Mind you, you don't know who came in immediately before you, and if you hadn't noticed who came in immediately after you, you're sunk. There's no receptionist and no appointments.

This system must cause some misunderstandings. The old ladies have it off pat. They're used to coming regularly (not like me). When somebody isn't sure about their turn they'll say, 'Was I in before you?' Now, how the Hell are you supposed to know that? It's like going into the Candy Shop and asking Mrs Robinson for a packet of Spangles and three of those sweets that man had a week gone Wednesday and expecting her to remember. I'm bound to get it wrong. I'm getting dead nervous now. There are three faces I'm nearly sure were in before me, or maybe four. I'm not sure about the old fellow with the warty nose and the deaf-aid. I mean, that's just it. You'd think I'd be sure about him, wouldn't you? He's the only one with a deaf-aid and a warty nose.

I know I'm going to make a cod of myself. There's twelve of us in here, and since Maggie and Grace have gone the place is as quiet as a confessional queue. You look up and catch the eye of the bloke in the flat cap and the grey gabardine coat, and he looks away sharp in case he has to speak. Why is he wearing his best cap and coat to go to the doctor's? (Clean underpants, yes.) But I bet the last time he wore that coat was going to the market hall dance over twenty years ago, by the look of it. I mean, the doctor isn't going to say, 'What a lovely coat, Mr Gregg, shame about the boil under your arm,' is he?

I think he's going to tell me it's just a strain, and not to do any heavy lifting till it goes back down. I think I must have got it humping the bags of taties at Andrew Watson's farm. Well, tatie-picking is over for this year, so I should recover fast, I hope.

CHAPTER 41
ONLY A DREAM
THEY'VE STARTED AGAIN

I'm in the Co-op at Maryport, of all places. (Dad always buys his pigeon food from here.) I find myself peeing in the front hall of the shop. People are watching me, but I can't help myself. One of the shop assistants spots me and calls me a dirty wee bugger, and hands me a hose pipe and a yard brush. Why is the shop floor on a steep slope? It falls away from the tatie counter to the cold meats. There's an old man on two sticks in a tatty brown trench coat tied around the middle with baling twine and wearing clogs. He slips in the stream of pee.

I'm just about panic-stricken and sweating like a pig. The hose pipe is spewing out gallons of water in every direction with the pressure of a fire-hydrant. I've flooded the whole shop. There's bags of sugar, boxes of tea, crates of soup and barrels of vinegar floating through the shop like flotsam and jetsam from a sinking ship, straight through the back doors and onto the main street. I see Pauline Howlett. She's laughing at me. Then I realise I'm naked. I tell her on passing, 'It gets worse.' She laughs again. My nakedness embarrasses me because I'm too skinny.

Mam says I'm having a growth spurt again. I'm like a Biafran. Six months ago I had the merest hint of pectoral muscles, but they've gone again only to be replaced by a wash-board chest. Dad says I'm going to be wiry like him. I don't want to look like 'Son of Gandhi', I want to be 'Son of Ben Hur', or 'Son of Hercules', or even, better still, 'Son of Samson'. Oh, well, I'm stuck with it for now, I suppose. Genes will out, or will they? I could get a bullworker and pump my body up like Charles Atlas. I don't want to look like Charles Atlas, I'd settle for a more sturdy version of me. Maybe when my current growth spurt stops I'll fill out again.

I find myself outside on the main street, but it's not Maryport any more, it's Cleator Moor High Street. Just about everybody I know from school is there standing peering out of the windows or standing in the doorways. The water is going right down the Clock Hill, past the Meadow Dairy and Walter Willsons, Hannah Thwaites' and the Westminster Bank; old men appearing out of Pat Curran's barbers, and the water continues down the hill to Carruthers's Cloggers and takes a sharp right into the coal yard. I'm completely bollock-naked.

I try to hide my modesty with my hand/hands (I'm more than a handful now!), and pray for the ground to open up and swallow me. Then, horror of horrors, I'm getting, you know, uncomfortable (I'm starting to sound like that Cistercian Monk!) and I'm still naked in front of all these people, who look away and pretend not to notice.

Suddenly, and very dramatically 'Drac' (Miss Cunningham) appears in a sort of SS-style uniform, complete with a cap, jodhpurs and hacking jacket and a whip. Then, just when I think I'm going to be discovered and shamed, I waken up to find myself PP and go to the toilet for a leak. I'm still shaking ten minutes later after I get back into bed.

How vivid some dreams are! You can recall every bizarre detail for ages after. Thank God it's only a dream.

CHAPTER 42
NAMED AND SHAMED

There's a great bit of drama going on at Church at the moment. I've taken to going to ten o'clock Mass, because there's more talent goes to ten than nine, and I've got a new suit. Nana Heron bought Stephen and me the new suits for our fourteenth birthday. Mine's a sort of sandy-brown colour; not orange exactly, but not far off. Straight jacket, no back vent or side vents, narrow lapels and three buttons, single breasted. Dead tight drain-pipe trousers. Stephen's is a sort of silver-grey shiny material, exactly the same style as mine. We look like the Everley Brothers.

There's nothing like a good suit for pulling the birds, even after Mass. You get the chance to weigh up the talent going to Communion and make sure you accidentally bump into them squeezing your way out of the throng leaving the Church through the small vestry door. After your apology you soon get to know if there's any interest and take it from there.

Mind you, I'm not saying it's the only reason I go to Mass. I love the Mass. I wouldn't dream of missing Mass, even if there wasn't a single bit of talent to be seen, but it's a lovely feeling to be dressed to the nines and mingling in a big crowd of people. A good suit gives you self-confidence and a comfortable body image; essential if you're on the pull.

Well, that's just by the bye, because the drama I'm talking about involves one of our priests, Father Mark. He's just a tad serious. I mean, even a priest should lighten up sometimes, but he never seems to; not to me, and I serve his Mass, so I should know. Well, his current mission isn't serving the starving babbies of Africa, or insisting women should still be obliged to cover their heads in Church as some priests still believe. No, his mission is much nearer to home. He's hell-bent on recovering all the Church debts. When I say Church debts I don't mean debts the church owes the people, I mean the debts other people owe the Church.

You see, Father McCann, God bless him, won't see anybody stuck. You don't have to be a Catholic either. He's famous for lending his parishioners, and others, money. He doesn't charge interest or anything like that, but he does expect to be paid back in a reasonable amount of time. Of course, he's left himself wide open to abuse and allegedly, according to Father Mark, many people just haven't bothered to repay him. So he's going to get it all back on Father McCann's behalf, although I think Father McCann is being coerced into this purge of the debtors. I secretly think he would rather prefer to let sleeping dogs lie.

The first hint of a public expose, to me at any rate, was the rather unusual end to Father Mark's homily. He made a mumbled reference to the fact that unfortunately some parishioners had so far not responded to a letter requesting everyone who owed the parish money to outline how they intended to pay it back.

The next week at ten o'clock Mass he dedicated a bit more time at the end of his homily to explaining that he had taken it upon himself to reduce the money owed to the parish because he firmly believed that people were purposely borrowing money without the slightest intention of ever paying it back. Then he very dramatically announced that he knew of a parish in the North East where a similar situation occurred and the parish priest had taken the unprecedented step of naming names from the pulpit and on the notice board at the back of said church.

This was a very controversial statement for a priest to make and people were very upset to be hearing this sort of talk from the pulpit. Well, upset or not, there was a very sudden shift of numbers from the congregation abandoning other Masses to attend ten o'clock Mass the following week, because Father Mark also announced his intention to give regular updates on his progress and further steps he intended to take to reverse the problem of bad debtors. He said it was crucial to retrieve the bad debts and to halt this trend to deceive Father McCann's trust.

CHAPTER 43
BLIND DATE

Talking about crucial, I know it's nothing to do with this crack, but it just reminds me of a really funny incident which took place last Friday night. Our Stephen has a girlfriend, well, more a dancing partner for the record hops and she comes from Frizington. Her name's Jean, and on Wednesday night he'd been talking to her about going to Wyndham School Social on Friday night and she said she had a mate who fancied me. So Steve wanted to know if I fancied a blind date to make up a foursome.

I think Jean's Mam would only agree to her going to Wyndham School Social if her mate was going as well, so although feeling rather apprehensive about a blind date, but being reassured by Stephen's description of Judith (that was my blind date's name), I agreed to go along with it. What the hell? If she's a real dog I can dump her and find my own chick when we get there. Nicely, mind you. I wouldn't hurt any lass's feelings. I'd let her down gently.

So Stephen had arranged to meet the lasses off the half-past six bus from Frizington at Wath Brow corner and get the twenty to seven bus to Egremont, which we did. While we were waiting for the Frizington bus, Stephen reassured me about Judith, saying she was small and dark, a bit quiet, but nice. Well, I wasn't convinced this wasn't a terrible mistake, but it was too late to back out now, so we waited.

Just before their bus was due to arrive the twenty past six bus to Frizington was leaving the bus stop and I noticed three elderly ladies coming round the corner from Greystone Road in a bit of a rush. The bus had started to move off by now and when it was on level with the women one of them managed to jump on, leaving her two mates running after the bus.

The bus was picking up a bit of speed, and the second lady, helped by the one already on the back platform, reached forward and grabbed the chrome pole. She almost managed to clamber onto the platform, but suddenly lost her grip and landed like a sack of taties onto the road. Her mate who was following her, and by now nearly doing a four-minute mile, ran into her and landed smack bang on top of her. Stephen and me were horrified. Suddenly, and without any warning, the third lady who was already on the bus, jumped off and landed with a hell of a thud onto the road.

Honest to God, it was like 'Emergency Ward 10'. There was blood and knickers everywhere. If it hadn't been so awful it would have been hysterical. Stephen and me and half a dozen other people helped the old ladies to their feet and somebody from Dent Aerated Water took the one who had scopped herself off the bus like a Kamikaze pilot into the office, and I think phoned for an ambulance. Stephen and me just looked at each other, and I don't know if it was shock or what, but we just collapsed into a fit of laughter. We just couldn't help it. We were so sorry for the poor women, but God! It was so bloody funny!

The lasses' bus from Frizington arrived on time and Jean, who I knew to look at stepped off the bus first, swiftly followed by this vision in black. She was small and dark with short black hair cut in the Italian boy's style. She was wearing a short black mini PVC Mac and white plastic knee boots and covering her head with a see-through plastic umbrella. Hell's fire! She looked like Suzy Wong from a few yards away. She even had the slitty eyes.

Stephen wasn't wrong. She was tidy, alright. Jean made the introductions and grabbed Stephen's arm and left me floundering with the every-so-shy Suzy Wong. I of course was still in a slight state of shock from having experienced seeing the three old ladies splattered on the road, so I initially started to tell Suzy about this and by the time we got on the bus the crack had practically dried up. It was like drawing teeth, but I blathered away nervously trying to extract something representing a conversation from her.

The bus to Egremont arrived not a minute too soon. I was sure I was going to say something really stupid in my attempt to keep the crack going. Well, after ascertaining who was her favourite group (Gerry and the Pacemakers) and what was her favourite dance (the Jive – well, that's good news for me, it's mine as well), I noticed she was carrying a small parcel with her and I asked her what she had in the parcel.

She said, 'It's a frock for my auntie.'

So I said, 'Why are you carrying it with you? You might lose it at the Social.' And she said she had to deliver it to her auntie's house, which is in Gully Flatts, before we go to the Social.

And I thought, 'Oh, great! We'll have to trail all the way to Gully Flatts and back into Egremont before we get to the Social, and if we don't get there before quarter past seven we won't get in.' I told her about my concerns and asked her if it was crucial, meaning was it crucial she delivered it before the Social, and she didn't seem to understand what I was saying (no change there, then). Then, after a moment of consideration and a quick look into the parcel, she looked at me and said, 'No, I think it's Crimplene.'

Well, I just cracked up. I burst out laughing. I mean, you couldn't make it up, you really couldn't. She looked shocked. Stephen, who was sitting on the seat in front of us poked his head over the back of the seat and saw me helpless with my head in my hands, bending over nearly touching the floor with my head in a vain attempt to control my laughing. Every time I thought about her answer I was off again.

Stephen said, 'What the hell's so funny?' and of course, I couldn't tell him. I just kept falling about. I honestly haven't laughed so much for God knows how long. 'Is it crucial?' 'No, I think it's Crimplene.' I just couldn't tell him. And when he asked Judith, she shrugged her shoulders and looked out of the bus window and said, 'Don't ask me, I think he's touched.' That just set me off again. I mean, she thinks I'm touched. That's rich coming from brain-dead Suzy Wong.

Well, things never really got off the ground between Judith (or Crucial, as Stephen and me christened her later). After that we escorted her to her auntie's to deposit her Crimplene frock and after we just made it in time to literally be the last four to be admitted to Wyndham Dance hall on account of it being full to capacity, she blew me out. She refused to dance with me and said I was a bloody nutter. Life just gets better and better.

Er, where were we? Oh, yes. Father Mark saying it's crucial (or was it Crimplene) that he recovered all the money owed in order to do urgent repairs to the Church. Things were hotting up. Two more weeks went by with maximum capacity gates at ten o'clock Mass, with Father Mark resembling some manic public relations officer who on the one hand was trying to get as much publicity for his cause, while on the other hand trying not to make it seem like a witch hunt, which of course it was.

He apparently had had a huge response from the debtors, but unfortunately there was still a small nucleus of people who had either refused to pay up or had not yet responded, and these people Father Mark was going to name and shame. They had exactly two weeks to pay up or he personally would read their names out from the pulpit at this ten o'clock Mass two weeks to the day, and afterwards the list would be pinned up in the Church porch for all to see.

Well, this was the subject of much debate. Had he any legal right to publicly name people who owed the church money? Could he prove they actually owed money? Would some of them sue him for defamation of character, or ultimately would Father McCann actually let him do the deed? These were all burning questions being asked by the whole congregation.

Come to think of it, Father McCann was keeping a very low profile. I hadn't seen him doing his round of the church during ten o'clock Mass in recent weeks. You don't suppose Father Mark has murdered him and wants to take over the parish for himself, do you? I mean, you read about these megalomaniacs who gain a bit of power and get carried away with it – look at Hitler! No, I'm just letting my imagination run away with me.

The next week's Mass was much of the same; one hundred per cent attendance capacity crowd and Father Mark saying a few people were still left to pay up. He said people must be wrestling with their consciences, so this was their last chance to lay all the ghosts. They had exactly seven days before he finally let everyone know who they were.

The final day came. I'm sure the Whitehaven News was there; well, everybody else was. The Church had not been so full since Father Clayton's funeral and the tension was electric. Five-past ten and no Father Mark. Everybody was focused on the vestry door.

Then suddenly the door opened. The acolytes slowly filed through the large pitch pine doors, all six of them, and then, bedecked in all his priestly glory, Father McCann strode out. A dull whisper rose from the congregation and a very uneventful Mass followed, Father McCann the celebrant. He got onto the pulpit to read the Gospel and instead of a homily he read a pastoral letter from the Bishop encouraging his flock to welcome and embrace the new Mass in English, which would be Canon Law by the end of the year.

Father Mark disappeared without trace, probably sent back to the Abbey or relocated to the Outer Hebrides or maybe the Scilly Isles. Father McCann might be a soft touch with money, but when it comes to his priests, he has the last say. He doesn't allow them any degree of autonomy.

CHAPTER 44
A TRIP TO KESWICK

May Day Monday, and an annual trip to Keswick was the order of the day. Jimmy Mac and Aunty Jean, Cousin Linda and James in Jimmy Mac's car; Mam, Dad, Stephen, Barry, Margaret and myself in the old silver Rover. We were all ready to set off from Croasdale Place when our young cousin, Geraldine, Aunty Lilly's eldest daughter, came up to the cars to show us a thrush's egg she'd found in the back garden.

I think she really wanted to come with us but there wasn't any room, and Mam said she wouldn't take one of the cousins and leave the rest, so she looked a bit pathetic. I wanted to move over and let her in, but Mam wound the window down and told her she was really sorry she couldn't take her with us, but it wouldn't have been fair on Raymond and Stephen and Diane, and gave her a kiss and half a crown to buy them all an ice cream later in the day. Geraldine pretended she didn't mind and thanked Mam for the money, then she handed me the thrush's egg and said, 'That's for you, Sean, for taking me on your bike.'

I took it from her and thanked her, wondering what I was going to do with it when Mam said, 'I'll take that and put it safe on the dashboard, Sean.' Then she must have pressed it too hard in her hand because it broke open and the contents seemed to hit every square inch of the car. It exploded and most of the contents went down the back of the front seat. It stank to high heaven. It was as rotten as a pear.

Well, there was pandemonium in the back of the car. All four of us dived for the doors to get away from the smell, it was really putrid. Mam and Dad clambered out, and as Dad went back into the house for some cloths and disinfectant Uncle Jimmy Mac came up to see what was going on. You can't imagine the smell. It was so strong inside the car Dad was baulking trying to clean it up. Jimmy Mac wasn't best pleased, because the time was getting on and he said we'd have to hurry if we were going to miss the heavy bank holiday traffic.

The smell was every bit as bad, except slightly sweeter because of the Dettol, when we piled back into the car. We all protested about the smell and Dad said, 'Don't take deep breaths and hang out of the window in turns,' as he left a faint strip of rubber on the tarmac. Mam said, 'For Christ's sake, Jay, they can't do that, they'll fall out!' You see, we'd had a bad experience with a car door once before.

It was years ago, when we lived at Cleator. We were all quite young, and there was Margaret, Stephen, Mam, Aunty May and me in the back of Papa's car. Nana and Papa were in the front. We were going down Inkerman Terrace into Whitehaven where there used to be a raised garden in front of one of the houses, which had Snow White and the Seven Dwarfs in a circle visible from the road. Actually it was even more visible from the bus, but you could see it clearly enough from the car if you were quick. Papa always slowed down to let us have a better view when we passed by.

For some reason Stephen always confused the name of Snow White with Nurse Benn, the local midwife (Freud, make sense of that!) and he shouted out, 'Look! There's Nurse Benn!' Well, Mam and Aunty May thought this was hysterical and started laughing. Stephen, realising his mistake, laughed and lurched to one side, accidentally pushing the door handle. The car door flew open and Stephen shot out. Like a flash Aunty May saw Stephen through the corner of her eye, and just managed to catch him by the foot. Papa, oblivious to this debacle, amid the hysteria continued to drive down Inkerman Terrace with Stephen bouncing up and down like a yoyo on Aunty May's arm.

Aunty May finally let go, just before the car stopped some two hundred yards or so from where he fell out. She could hold him no longer. Stephen rolled onto the road and back into the car and the back wheels rolled over his jacket, which by this time was only over one arm. He'll never be as lucky again. Amazingly he had only cuts and bruises on his hands and arms where he had tried to stop his head from hitting the road, but what a state everybody was in!

We set off with Dad in front, Jimmy Mac following at a safe distance behind. Well, we hadn't got to Park Side when I said, 'Mam, I'm going to be sick!'

She said, 'Jay, pull over, quick!'

Well, I got out of the car and threw three days' meals up on the grass verge. I'm always car-sick, but usually a few hours into a day out, not half a mile like I had just been. I really didn't want to get back into the car, because I knew I wasn't finished being sick and the smell was bound to make me sick again. Anyway, not wanting to dwell on the subject, I was sick seventeen times from our house to Portinscale and by this time Mam was getting a bit worried. She told Dad I'd better not get back into the car again, because I was just retching, there was nothing left to come up.

As we were on the south side of the lake it was decided to have our picnic near the lake edge and maybe, after some fresh air and some food we'd all feel a bit better, even though I was the only one being sick, nobody was enjoying the trip because of the smell. I did soon pick up, but just the thought of getting back into the car was enough to make me have a relapse, so Mam decided we should catch the launch into Keswick and leave our car in Portinscale. Jimmy Mac, however, decided he'd carry on to Grange and round the lake and meet up with us later.

The launch journey was great – all that fresh air, and after disembarking at Keswick and a short game of obstacle golf, Dad announced we were going to hire a motor boat and the six of us were going to have a trip to the island in the middle of the lake. These things always seem a good idea at the time, don't they?

We excitedly made our way to the jetty and eventually, after twenty minutes' wait, clambered aboard our put-put bound for Seagull Island, Dad at the helm looking like Captain Cook discovering Australia. We were all in our Sunday Best; the lads in our brogue shoes, grey flannels and white shirts, Stephen and me in our best Hawaiian ties. Thankfully we'd left our jackets in the Rover, because it was quite warm. Dad, however, had his jacket on because he never felt too warm, even when the sun splits the trees, which it nearly was this day. Mam was in her white pill-box hat, blue duster coat and white stiletos; Margaret in her pink twin set and baby-doll heeled shoes. Things didn't bode well.

The man at the jetty told Dad to keep twenty feet away from the shore at all times and not to let anybody stand up once we set off. We set off at just about a land walking pace and it felt really exciting, if maybe a bit staid, speed-wise. Once we'd passed the first headland and were heading into open waters we hardly seemed to make any progress at all. The wind had picked up in the open water and Mam was holding onto her hat. Dad decided to detour round the first island and keep near to the shore to avoid the wind, which was forcing a strong spray over us all.

Then, just when Dad changed direction for Seagull Island, it happened. We were about ten yards from the shore and suddenly we ran aground, or at least the front of the boat was stuck, and so Dad slammed the engine in reverse and nothing happened. We seemed to be stuck fast. The engine was roaring but we weren't moving. Mam was panic-stricken and Dad was telling her to settle herself and not to be so stupid. She was shouting at him for getting so near the shore and Margaret was just about hysterical.

There was only one thing for it. Some of us would have to get into the lake and push the boat free. All three of us wanted to get into the water, but Mam wasn't for it. Dad said, 'Right, Eileen. You sit back and shut up; I'll sort this out,' and told all three of us to take our shoes and socks, pants and shirts off and get into the water, which we hurriedly did. It was absolutely freezing, but we didn't care: we were on a rescue mission.

With Mam and Margaret huddled together in the rear of the boat and Dad in the middle, we tried to push the thing off the gravel bank, but even with our best efforts we couldn't move it. Mam was in a panic by now and clinging onto Margaret and her hat for grim death, so Dad jumped off the boat fully clothed, including his shoes, and swam round to the front, where we all gave a huge heave and the boat lurched backwards, Dad only just managing to keep hold of it, and clambering back over the side.

He soon pulled us onto the boat and headed away from the shore to safer depths of water. He was like a drowned rat. The only dry item of clothing he had was his jacket, which he'd slung off before he jumped into the water. We, however, took our wet vests and underpants off and hurriedly put our other clothes back on and were soon warm, but poor Dad was freezing. The ferry man wanted to know what happened, and Dad said, 'Mind your own business. I paid for the boat and that's all you need to know,' and ushered us off the boat onto dry land.

We then had to wait another half an hour for the ferry back to Portinscale which would have to go the full circuit of the lake before finally reaching Portinscale, by which time Dad was nearly dry. Jimmy Mac was waiting where we'd left the Rover and Dad and Jimmy went for a pint in the Portinscale Hotel while Mam told the whole sorry story to Aunty Jean, who thought it was hysterical.

Mam's hat was still intact.

When we finally got into the car and ready to set off back home Mam was smoking a cigarette. We all looked at her in amazement. Barry said, 'Mam, I didn't know you knew how to smoke a cigarette.' And she said, 'After a day like today, Barry, I could smoke a pipe, never mind a cigarette.'

It looked really odd, seeing Mam smoke. We'd never seen her smoke before and she entertained us all the way back home. I'd forgotten about the bad egg smell in the car; I was fascinated with Mam's new habit. Do you know, that smell stayed in the car for the duration. It never ever fully disappeared, in spite of Mam's best efforts with bleach and caustic soda.

When Dad finally had to let the car go (it went to Goodfellow's scrap yard at Cleator) because of its appetite for petrol, some twelve miles to the gallon on a long run, we were all very sad because it had style. Every trip in it was an occasion. Mind you, Dad hardly ever used it because of its petrol-guzzling, so the new set of wheels, although not so grand, was much cheaper to run. He bought a second-hand Bedford van. It was like a tank, and Dad rubbed it down and hand painted it royal blue. You could pick him out in a traffic jam of a thousand cars no bother. We christened it 'the blue portaloo', which wasn't a bad description, actually, after a month or so in Dad's possession.

CHAPTER 45
A YELLOW MINI/THE MCNAMEES

The pleasant walk from our house to St Mary's Church takes in the whole cross section of people living their lives out in various degrees of harmony in the houses on either side of the route. You walk from Seaview Place where we live (without a sea view), along Priory Drive, passing New Todholes Road and Victoria Villas, where the McNamees live.

The McNamees are a very prominent Cleator Moor Catholic family, one of the teaching families. Mrs McNamee, who is in her eighties, was a teacher at Saint Patrick's School. She taught three generations of children, Mam says. There was another lady called Mrs Richardson who also lives there, and an elderly man and a younger woman called Josephine who is also a teacher.

Dad does some decorating for them and the house is just like a shrine to the saints, and in the hall there's a picture of the sacred heart with a red candle which has been lit constantly for the last forty-five years, since they first moved into the house.

I know these things because I've been in the house helping Dad. They're very Irish-posh and very interested in our family; at least, they all ask questions about how old you are, and how's your grandmother and how many of my relatives they have taught. The list is endless. I feel slightly intimidated by their questions. Although they seem genuinely interested, I always get the impression that there's a hidden agenda.

Josephine, the strange younger woman says she went to school with my mother, and always enquires about her state of health, almost as if she's obsessed by peoples' health. It's hard to explain, but she looks at you too closely. I feel embarrassed by her stares.

Once, when I'd gone round to get the garden keys from Dad so I could feed the hens she was there, and I remember looking at her and thinking how I'd seen her in her car, parked in a bit of a funny place. It was in a gateway on the fell road, just parked there alone. She drove a yellow mini and wore very glamorous clothes and smelled of strong perfume, which always made me sneeze.

She greeted me and said to Dad, 'Here's your son, Mr Close. I hope he hasn't come to take you away.'

And Dad said, 'No, lass. He's come to get me keys for the hen garden, I bet.'

And she seemed to come alive, because sometimes she seemed to be in a world of her own, almost as if she didn't notice anybody around her. She wanted to know all about Dad's other jobs; how wonderful it must be to be part of a lovely family who looked after each other, she said; how lucky and blessed Mrs Close was ('Mrs Close'? Not 'Eileen', with whom she had gone to school and sat next to in lessons). By this time Mrs McNamee had appeared from one of the downstairs rooms and, in a very animated way, joined in with Josephine's litany of compliments about our lovely family.

Then, out of the blue, Josephine went very silent and seemed to be staring at me, and she said in a slight whisper to Mrs McNamee, 'He's so beautiful, and so young, isn't he?'

And Mrs McNamee agreed and they carried on the conversation, looking at me and talking as if I wasn't able to hear them. I wanted to crawl into a hole. Dad could see how awkward I felt and hurriedly passed me the garden keys. 'I'll have to get on with my duties,' I said to him to relieve the embarrassment I felt at being talked about in this way by these very caring, but very strange women.

Within a year of this encounter with the McNamees I was to learn that Josephine had been found dead, and Mam seemed to think that there was something suspicious about her death, and what a waste of a life hers had been. She never seemed to have found any real happiness or purpose to her life. Maybe she had decided to end it all and go to her father in heaven, where she knew she would eventually go.

The footpath leading from the McNamees' house leads to Saint Mary's Church and Grotto, which is just a short walk, and somehow seems to be the perfect place for a very special family to live. Next to Victoria Villas where the McNamees and the Richardsons lived was the Manse, the large impressive 1920s style house which was the home of the Methodist Minister and his wife. They kept themselves to themselves. Mind you, they couldn't be blamed for that – they were absolutely surrounded by Catholics.

The Manse and Victoria Villas had stood in glorious isolation for many a year, with a splendid view of Dent Mountain with nothing between the mountain and Hen Beck but rolling fields. Then in the late 1950s a huge council estate enveloped them from the sides and the rear and the new Saint Cuthbert's Catholic School popped up right in front of them, hemming them in from all quarters. What a nightmare that must have been for the rather reserved residents of these sleepy villas.

They stuck out like a sore thumb, and yet they were there first. The new council estate had street names like 'Clayton Avenue' and 'Brierley Road' and 'Holden Place', all named after Catholic priests from the parish. I wonder what the non-Catholic population made of it. It must have been like having salt rubbed into a wound. The Irish lot were having streets named after them – that must have taken some swallowing.

There is still an undercurrent of bitterness between the Catholics and Protestants, although, according to Mam and Dad, nothing like it had been in their younger days. Things have a way of levelling out when people learn to live with each other's different ways, and Cleator Moor was certainly trying very hard to do that.

CHAPTER 46
OUR BARRY'S Y-FRONTS

It was one of those morning again when you're off school and you haven't got your head round just what you're going to spend the day doing. It was a few weeks ago, and I had just rolled out of bed, pretending to myself that I'd fallen out. I was lying on the cool oilcloth between the two beds in our bedroom and it was a bit of a squeeze.

I was just thinking it's a good job we've got a bathroom, because where would we put a po in this bedroom? I mean, you couldn't put it too near to the door for fear of somebody kicking it over, and there certainly wasn't room between the beds because I could just fit with a squeeze, lying on my side.

I'm thinking these thoughts because I've been up in the night for a pee, a thing I never do, but I'd been drinking lemonade the night before. We'd skipped supper; Mam had said she just couldn't be bothered making sandwiches, so we could all have a packet of crisps and some lemonade for a wee change. Well, I must have drunk a pint of lemonade at least, so it woke me up in the early hours. That's when I heard Dad having a pee in the po in their bedroom, and it struck me that he hadn't got out of the habit of using the po instead of the toilet.

I mean, the toilet was only yards away, and yet he preferred to pee in the po next to the bed. I suppose it's easier to just slide your feet out of bed and perch yourself on the edge and let fly. I mean, you don't even have to stand up. But, like I say, you couldn't do that in our bedroom.

Why the hell am I bothering myself about where to park a bloody po? I mean, we'll never ever need one again. Dad still uses his, but only out of choice. I must stop concerning myself about things that don't matter. I am a bit of a worrier, you know.

When I finally upend myself and stagger aimlessly past the dressing table en route to the bathroom (or should I use the po in Mam and Dad's room?), I catch a full frontal view of myself in the mirror. I've got my white cotton underpants on, with the long legs and the button flies – no vest because it had been a warm night. I am acutely aware of my body image.

I am reasonably happy with what I see; I am slim in build, I have good defined muscles in my upper arms, and my shoulders, although not yet muscular, are reasonably broad. My chest has a way to go, but it's getting there, and because I've spent a few days sunbathing with my new radio in the back garden I am a pleasing olive brown colour.

I strike a pose, you know, the way body-builders do, but it makes me look ridiculous. I stand slightly to the side, bend my left knee slightly and form a fist with my right hand. I think there must be a knack to this and I certainly don't have it. I'm gaining self-confidence on the beach in my trunks, though. I think the suntan definitely helps. These underpants are pretty gross, I'm thinking. I've only had them on for a few days but already they need to be changed.

You see, I don't usually sleep in them. Until recently we've always slept in pyjamas, but I like the firmness and support around the wedding tackle, it feels more comfortable, so I should change them more often. With this in mind I drop my pants and open the top drawer of the dressing table. You know how your mind wanders.

I'm smiling to myself at something one of the lads said in the changing rooms at school the other day. I think it was Brian Graham. Somebody was doing a check for the most skiddies in the underpants, and one pair had been singled out as being two-thirds covered. The crotch from hell, we named him. Anyhow, Brian had told skiddy-crotch that the best way to check if your underpants needed changing was to throw them at the wall and if they fell to the ground they were good for a couple more days. If they stuck to the wall they definitely needed changing. Mine aren't anything like that. Just the odd drop of body fluid.

The top drawer of the dressing table contains all our underwear, Stephen's, Barry's and mine. Three separate piles of underpants, vests and socks. Barry seems to have more of everything than Stephen and me, probably because he's just back from the junior seminary and he needs more underwear because they only get washed once a week. Mam seems to wash everything every day, so we don't need so many. Anyhow, one pair of underpants at the top of Barry's pile catches my eye. They look different; just as white as all the rest, but a different style.

When I pick them up I can see they're the new style Y-front

underpants. I decide to try them on, and hurriedly step into them. They feel really comfortable; no legs in them, just a nice snug fit. They seem to sort of draw your eyes into the middle section, where the bulge is neatly contained. I reckon I looked half decent in these swish underkecks and take a final admiring look at myself, when from nowhere, Barry walks into the bedroom.

Straight away he notices the Y-fronts and shouts at me to take them off. I tell him I'm only trying them on, and he says, 'Well you can just take them off and give them to Mam straight away to wash.' I tell him I've only had them on for a couple of minutes, and he says he doesn't care. He's not wearing them again until they've been washed. I hurriedly remove the Y-fronts and replace them with a pair of my usual old-fashioned underpants and curse him for being so fussy. Stephen wouldn't mind me wearing his underpants, in fact half the time we wear each other's anyway.

When I took the Y-fronts to Mam and told her about Barry's outburst she said his behaviour would be because he was used to having his own underclothes at the boarding school and wasn't used to sharing his things like Stephen and me were. I understood what she was saying, but I couldn't see me reacting in the same way with my brothers, no matter how unused to sharing my things I had become. He's better off away from the junior seminary if they encourage people not to share their things.

Well, it looks as if he's not going back because he told me last night he's hoping to start at the Grammar School in Whitehaven next term. He doesn't really want to talk about the de la Salle brothers, so I'm not going to press him on the subject. He was obviously unhappy and probably just wanted to come back home. He was only twelve when he went away and it's a bit young to be making plans for your entire future.

Anyhow, after three years I suppose he's had time to realise whether or not the life was for him and decided against it. Now the family is complete once again, and a good thing too. Mam must be secretly delighted.

CHAPTER 47
DAD'S LEFT SELLAFIELD FOR GOOD

My Dad was never out of work. He's spent most of his adult life, after being demobbed from the army in 1945, working at Sellafield. All of his jobs were on the construction site, employed by firms like Taylor Woodrow and Matthew Hall.

He worked for a brief spell with BNFL on process work, but didn't like it. These were all multi-national companies and good payers, but years of labouring and chopping and changing jobs all on the Sellafield site had made him weary. Too many ghosters and double shifts had given him stomach ulcers. The long hours and the irregular meals were making him a very sick man.

He was no longer fit for heavy shift work, so, being a man who could easily adapt himself to new situations, he embarked on a new career. He went into partnership with his mate, Charlie McGrady and they started a window cleaning business. He'd had a part-time window cleaning round when he worked at Sellafield; he worked between shifts and on his days off, so he knew there was a living to be made from it. He could be home every day for his midday meal and finish on time for a dinner at five o'clock every night. This would be much better for his general health and was to prove to be a great source of crack at the dinner table.

Mam was worried at first, always having been sure of a regular wage packet before – although it was contract work it was always regular – and now wondering how Dad would manage during the bad weather. She needn't have worried because Dad got loads of decorating jobs to do as a spin-off from the windows which he kept for the wet days, and all would be well.

Sometimes, if Dad had been rained off for a few hours early in the day and the weather got back out again later, he would do a few windows in the evenings, and I used to go with him to lend a hand moving his ladders and fetching him clean water. I used to enjoy these odd shifts with Dad.

One evening after school Dad announced that he'd *do a few of the pubs* tonight. 'Sean, do you fancy giving me a hand?' and I jumped at the chance. I'd been before with Dad when he was *doing a few of the pubs* and we always ended up in Danny McMullen's on Bowthorn

Road. Dad would have a couple of pints and I'd have a lemonade and some crisps and listen to the crack in the snug. Danny's was a good pub; a proper pub with good regulars. He also had a good snug where his most famous patron, Councillor John Colligan, used to hold court.

On this particular night we'd done the Derby Arms, the Golden Lion, the Queen's Arms, the Globe Hotel, the Commercial and the Wheatsheaf and Dad had had a half-pint in each and we'd finished, as usual, at Danny McMullen's at about half past eight. The ladders were secured onto the bogey and we ensconced ourselves for a nice wee session. Kids weren't really allowed into the bar, but if I kept quiet and nobody objected I was allowed in the snug with Dad.

When we arrived, John Colligan had already assumed his usual chair facing the bar and a collection of regulars were in position ready to debate the latest news items and pontificating on how to run the country and prevent the current spate of law-breaking and insubordinations. This would be interspersed with a few impromptu unaccompanied songs; anything from Danny Boy to Barefoot Days and My Brother, Sylvest.

Some of the local Bowthorn ladies patronised Danny's snug and I used to just sit tucked away in a corner at the end of the bar on a high stool and immerse myself in the humour and wisdom of these wonderful people. John Colligan, as well as being a councillor and all-round good egg, was a school teacher. He was in the habit of late of having his evening meals at Danny's and rounding the day of with a few of the landlord's finest ales. He was always attired in his smart suit and a dickie-bow tie. This was his trademark.

There was a handful of regulars in the snug when we arrived, but by half past nine it was getting full. Dad was talking to Jack Fleming, an old neighbour of ours from Cleator, when Mattie Rogan burst in. Mattie was a resident of Bowthorne Road; a middle-aged matronly woman with a badly lamed leg. She was a respectable, well-liked and colourful character, who liked a glass of whisky and was a regular devotee of Danny's. She was accompanied by another keen devotee of Danny's, Rita Zarjac and her husband, Waddy, a Pole. They shuffled and squeezed their way into their regular seats, which nobody else ever occupied, and got themselves dug in for the night.

Rita said, 'Go on, Mattie, tell them about your Buster.'

And John said, 'What's that, Mattie?'

'Well,' she says, 'John, you wouldn't believe the day I've had today. It's a miracle I've made it here at all.'

'Get away,' says John. 'What's to do, then?'

'Well,' starts Mattie, still breathless from her walk the full length of Bawthorn Road to the pub. 'It must have been about five-and-twenty minutes past nine this morning, because I was getting ready for that twenty-to-ten bus to the Moor and I was putting me coat on ready when one of Rooney's lads shouted through me back door, 'Have you lost your dog, Mrs Rogan?' Well, I hadn't noticed whether Buster was in or out; you know what he's like, Rita, he just comes and goes willy-nilly.'

'Aye, lass,' says Rita comfortingly.

'So I shouts up the stairs and into the lobby, 'Buster, Buster!', but no sign of him in the house. So I shouted to Rooney's lad, "Why, what's he supposed to have done now?" Well, the poor wee bugger didn't know what to say and I said, "Come on, lad, what's the matter? – thinking he'd been after his father's hens. And he said – my God, I'm shuddering just thinking about it – "He's been run over down the dibb, at least I think it's your dog, Mrs Rogan".'

'Well, Rita, me blood ran cold.'

'Oh, Mattie, lass, it must have,' said Rita, holding onto Mattie's hand while she took a wee sip of her whisky and continued.

'So I says to him, "What colour is it, lad?"'

'And he says, "It's a brown and white whippet." Well, me legs just went from under me, Rita,' says Mattie.

'Oh, Mattie! Oh, mother of God! That's terrible,' says Rita with such high drama.

'So I picks me camel coat off the arm of the sofa and trundles all the way down to the dibb.' The whole snug was silent and hanging on to her every word.

'The tears is blinding me, John – I love the bones of that wee dog.' Rita's nearly inconsolable by this time, with Mattie comforting her by now.

'Well, sure enough, he's there, as dead as a nit and bleeding like a pig; everybody's offering their condolences. So I wrapped him up in me camel coat and carried him back home. The coat's covered in blood, Rita, I'll have to have it cleaned.'

'Well, that's nowt, lass,' says Rita. 'At least it will clean. It's a bonny coat, that, Mattie.'

'So our Eddy comes in from first shift,' says Mattie, 'and buries him in the back garden. I took his lead and two tins of dog food and threw them in the dustbin and swore I'll never have another dog to break me heart. Then, about four o'clock, I goes out to lait some sticks out for the fire in the back shed, and the next thing, this bloody whippet bounds down the yard past me and into the house. Well, John, I was gobsmacked!'

'Aye, lass, you must have been,' says John. 'It couldn't have been Buster, though, your Eddy had just buried him, hadn't he?'

'Aye, but it wasn't Buster he'd buried,' says Mattie with a wee laugh. 'God knows whose bloody dog he buried, we've tried to find out, but come up with nowt yet. I couldn't believe it, Rita.'

Rita's looking as is she's just won Father McCann's sweep, smiling like a vision, and hanging on to every word Mattie was saying. 'I charged in after him and picked him up, checking it really was Buster, and kissing the face off him at the same time. I says to him, "Where have you been, you wee tyke? I thought you were dead! But now you've come back to me I don't care if you piss all over the house." Nor I don't, Rita, I'm just delighted to have him back, but somebody's missing a wee pet tonight and they're probably trailing the streets as we speak, God help them,' says Mattie.

Rita has held her peace, not wanting to steal Mattie's thunder, but as soon as she feels a decent space of time has been spent on Mattie's tale she launches into a crack of her own. She says, 'Here, do you mind when Waddy's cock chicken got squashed by that steam roller on our fronts when they were re-laying the road?'

Wilf Rogers says, 'Away to hell out of that, Rita.'

'Yes,' says Rita. 'Honest to God. The poor bugger (Waddy, that is), he'd been fattening it up for months and it had a belly like a poisoned pup. It was well on the way to a good fifteen pounds for Christmas, but it wasn't to be.'

She wore an expression of pathos and held it for a short while before continuing, 'It must have got out of the back garden and come through the house. We knew nowt about it until the council man knocked on the front door and says to Waddy, "Is this your hen?" Well, poor Waddy traipsed through into the kitchen and scops the cock chicken onto the table and says to me 'Can you make owt with this?' I says, 'What the hell is it?' ' to Mattie, who's now fully recovered from her ordeal and enjoying the nice wee tale from Rita, and grinning and chuckling away.

'Aye,' she says. 'Go on.'

'Well, Mattie, there wasn't enough left on it for a decent pan of soup. It was as flat as a fluke. Well, you would be, wouldn't you, with a ten ton steam roller over your face,' said Rita in her dead-pan style.

'Aye, Rita,' says John. 'Some terrible tragedies have befallen you in your day, lass,' and lifts his paper up to regale the snug with a synopsis of the day's political events.

Meanwhile, the ladies are having a more personal conversation. Mattie asks Rita how she's doing after her operation and the rest of the crack is conducted in what appears to me to be coded messages. 'Well,' says Rita, 'It's been five weeks, lass, and I managed me first wee night out at the Working Men's last Friday.'

'Oh, good, good. I'm pleased for you, lass,' says Mattie.

'Aye, but things'll never be the same, Mattie.'

'No, lass,' says Mattie. 'Just bide your time. God's good.'

'Aye, well I pray to Saint Anthony every night, Mattie and to Saint Jude,' says Rita.

'Well have you tried Saint Martin?' says Mattie. 'I swear by Saint Martin, lass. He's never let me down.'

'Oh, well,' says Rita, 'I'll give him a go. Our Sadie likes Saint Martin.' Then a sort of healing silence occurs between the two ladies for a few minutes, until at last Rita announces to the whole snug, 'You know the song 'Why not take all of me'?'

And Nellie Rooney answers, 'Aye, lass.'

'Well, that's what I think they've done, or they might as well have when I had that operation,' again in her dead pan style, received by her audience with great mirth. She'd apparently had it all taken away.

She continues to entertain the room. 'I have to laugh. It's stopped my gallop, right enough. You know, poor Waddy, wasn't for me going to the Working Men's so soon after me operation, but I said,

"To hell, Waddy, you're a long time dead, lad." So we goes. Well, I'm enjoying meself, and far from ready to go home when Waddy says, "Rita, it's after midnight, lass, we should be making our way home, it's late enough for you." So I says, "Aye away to hell out of that, Waddy, I'm not ready for home yet. You go if you like, I'll follow with our Sadie".'

'So I loses all track of time, John, you know what it's like. The crack was good and I'm enjoying me wee drink, so when I finally gets home. It's after two o'clock and Waddy's in bed. So I sneaks me clothes off in the kitchen so as not to disturb him and makes me way upstairs. I opens the bedroom door and he's snoring his scope off. I can see the moon reflecting off his baldy head, God love him. So I tries to climb over him to get to my side of the bed and lands slap bang on top of him.'

Meanwhile everybody's listening with great interest and some disbelief. 'The poor bugger! He wakens and nearly necks himself thinking he's being attacked!'

And John Colligan's laughing at the tale and says, 'Get away out of that, Rita.'

And she says, 'No, honest to God, John. So I rolls over onto my place and says, 'For God's sake, Waddy, will you settle, you nearly frightened the life out of me.' And the poor bugger says, 'Sorry, lass, I must have been dreaming.' I don't deserve him. Honestly, I really don't deserve him.'

Well, the crack had been good, but Dad's the other side of seven or eight pints of Hartley's bitter, of which he says, 'If God made anything better in this world he's kept it for himself'. So, we've got a bogey full of ladders to push up Leckonfield Hill and I know who's going to be doing the lion's share of the pushing. I say to Dad, 'Do you think we should be making tracks, Dad? We've got the bogey, remember.'

And he says, 'Aye, lad, you're right. We'd better not get too settled or you'll never get the bogey up that hill.'

CHAPTER 48
A UFO OR I'LL EAT MY HAT

It was a dark, cold, frosty winter's night. It must have been early February. The days were getting longer, but it was still getting dark about half past six. We'd had our teas, Malcolm Tate and me, and we were doing nothing special on the car park, just having the crack. We'd taken shelter from the cold winds between two garages, when it happened.

At first I thought the sound was from a tractor in Abe Woodburn's field, and I could see Malcolm staring past me above my head. A strange light was shining on him and I could see every strand of hair on his head. For a moment I didn't question in my mind why I could see him so clearly in the dark, only, what was he looking at? I slowly turned my head in the direction Malcolm was so intensely focused on and was nearly blinded by the bright light. The noise was getting louder and neither Malcolm or myself could move a limb. We were transfixed.

I remember thinking, 'Why don't we run away? There's nothing stopping us.' But we didn't. The noise wasn't like anything I'd ever heard before; it wasn't a regular engine noise, like a helicopter, it was much more high pitched and constant. The only sound I can describe it as being similar to is that of a lift falling at high speed.

The light focused on us for several minutes and the sound stayed constant. I couldn't see anything except the strong light, which seemed to have a narrow beam directed at us. I could only see blackness surrounding the light until very suddenly it moved away from us. As it quickly moved away and across the sky I could see its outline very briefly, and it seemed to be silver in colour and shaped like a fat cigar.

Malcolm looked at me and said in a low voice, 'What the hell was that?'

I answered, 'God knows! But what ever it was, it was interested in us.'

Neither of us felt particularly shaken by the experience. We moved out into the open space of the car park and looked to see if there was anybody else about who had seen what we'd just seen, not fully convinced we'd actually seen what we'd seen. Within seconds of our moving into the open car park from in between the garages where we had just been standing, there appeared the most singularly hideous sight I had ever seen, or indeed, have ever seen since.

A fireball creature was squealing and writhing in agony. It dropped to the ground, still on fire and curled up in a ball. We both ran together to see what it was and lying in front of us was a dead cat, it's fur completely burned off and a stench of singed fur and petrol or spirits of some sort hung in the air. We were horrified. This had been a more frightening sight than the one we'd just seen. The cat had died in absolute agony; its bare skin was burnt black and one of its eyes was burned out.

I don't know which one of us had the idea first, but we decided to go to the police station and report the dead cat. We didn't discuss the previous experience with each other on the way, or to the policeman at the station. He told us that had been the third report in less than a month of cats being covered with petrol and set alight. He questioned us about what we were doing on the car park in the dark, and whether we had heard or seen anything suspicious, like noises in the field or voices before or after we saw the cat.

We both said we'd heard nothing, and he said, 'Are you sure? You don't have to be afraid to report these lads, they need to be stopped. It's a terrible cruel thing they're doing, you know.' We were both adamant we hadn't seen or heard anything, we just saw the cat shoot out from behind the garages. The policeman said we must come back if we remembered anything out of the ordinary, and to get off home, we'd obviously had a nasty shock. (You could say that.)

Later on in the week, the Whitehaven News reported several sightings of a flying saucer over Cleator Moor and Keekle on the previous Monday night, and gave this very tongue-in-cheek report from five separate eye witnesses. Malcolm and me were both reluctant to discuss what we had seen. I think we hoped that by not talking about it we could pretend it didn't really happen. Was the cat set alight by cruel, uncaring yobs, or was there some other explanation?

That night I had a dream, and in that dream I found myself being coerced by demons. The dream was all mixed up, of course, but the thread that ran through it was forcing me to forget my recent experience and not to speak of it to anyone. I succeeded in this for many years, and when the fear finally left me I was able to recollect all the details.

CHAPTER 49
BOBBY'S GIRL

I'm sure that's why all the lasses were after him. Just because he's called Bobby.

Brenda Lee's *Bobby's Girl* was heading for the Christmas Number One spot, and everybody was singing it, and Bobby Smith was like the cat that got the cream. Jacqueline Sharp and Cecilia Keenan were breaking into it at the drop of a hat on every possible occasion. Our classroom, 2A, in Christmas week 1960, was bedecked with paper streamers; the windows were covered in cotton-wool snow and painted Father Christmases. It was a non-uniform week. Let the carnival commence!

And carnival it was. We were hyped up to hell. For the last two days we were allowed to take board games into school, have class quizzes and generally mess about in a controlled sort of way. It was like Sodom and Gomorrah, or so it seemed. Mistletoe was sneaked in and hung above the broom cupboard door purposely, so that a chance kiss could lead to a full-blown snog, tongues and the lot, in the semi-privacy of the broom cupboard.

Bobby was one of the hard men; tall and well-built, teddy boy hair style and an attitude to match. That was on the surface; he was a good laugh, really, not half as hard as he made out. I got on great with him. Most of the lads had coifs and DAs (DA is short for 'duck's arse', requiring the back of the hair to be combed from each side into the centre) held in place with Brylcreem, or in our Stephen's case, Vaseline, him having thick, straight hair. My coif fell naturally into a huge cone shape, almost touching my nose. It looked like a round, soggy shredded wheat.

What, with my impossibly tapered black trousers, white polo-neck sweater and two-tone brown winkle-picker shoes, I was showing early indications of becoming a fashion victim, but what the hell, it was Christmas!

Your first Christmas as a teenager – that has got to be the best Christmas of all time. None better before and certainly nothing to match it after. I was a Second Year, fully initiated into school life, with a hairstyle to die for, not a spot in sight and a handful of first year lasses chasing after me. I thought I was the goods. There's only one way to go from here, and that's down.

All the crack in the classroom was about the Christmas party on Wednesday night, followed by the record hop and a select few, myself and Stephen included, had been invited to a party during the holidays at Ray Woods's house. His Mam and Dad were going to go out and let him have a party. My God! I couldn't see Mam letting us have a party. In fact, Stephen had suggested it to her a few days earlier and her answer was, 'Aye, of course you can, when Nelson gets his eye back!' When pressed further she replied, 'Not on your bloody life!' I think that was a 'No'.

The school Christmas party was, of course, in the school hall. After the buffet (don't ask me what it consisted of, the food was on no interest to me; I was waiting for the action that followed), all the lads and lasses cleared the tables and stacked them to one side, placing the chairs around the perimeter of the hall. Ma Murphy started the proceedings by placing an LP on the record deck on stage. The music was amplified by the loud-speakers round the hall and the Old Time and Barn Dancing section began.

We did the Barn Dance, the Military Two-Step, the Gay Gordons, the Schottische, an Irish Reel and a Scottish Square Dance. The girls wore jive frocks with wide skirts and paper nylon underskirts to give them body. They had bright, shining faces and pony tails. By this time next year they would be wearing mini skirts and halter neck skinny ribbed tops and their eyes would be as black as pandas. It would all happen as quick as that.

After the Old Time came the up-to-date stuff. Jiving to Elvis's *Jail House Rock*, Chubby Checker's *Let's Twist Again*, Chris Montez's *Let's Dance*, and of course, *Bobby's Girl*, with Bobby Smith pushed into the middle of the floor chased by a bevy of second-year beauties.

When the smooching records came on, *Sealed With A Kiss*, *Unchained Melody* and *Tell Laura I Love Her*, Ma Murphy, Mr Pattinson and Mr Singleton were on call, gently tapping on the shoulders of any couple who were smooching too close together, putting an arm between them to indicate the requisite distance deemed decent, and anybody found snogging was put out of the hall. No bad thing, really, because you could continue with the high passion in the cloakrooms and even manage a bit of a grope, if you were lucky.

This was the start of my obsession with pop music, pop records and record hops. It probably wasn't a real obsession, because for a start

I couldn't afford to buy many records. Our paper round delivering the Barrow Mail nightly provided Stephen and me with enough pocket money to buy some top ten singles, and even enough to gain entry to the scout hut record hop on Wednesday nights, the Ehenside record hop on Thursday nights and Saint Cuthbert's record hop on Friday nights. Plus bottles of Vimto and packets of crisps.

We somehow managed to finance our entire social life and keep pace with the trends without having to ask Mam and Dad for a single penny. We could even manage the Hip on a Saturday night as well, so there wasn't much time left for homework. We did the bare necessity and managed to scrape through.

These record hops were becoming more popular and more permissive as the pop records became more suggestive and risqué. Ehenside and the scout hut hops were the best. They were the flesh-pots of Cleator Moor for us. The smooch was allowed, even a bit of a snog on the dance floor was tolerated, but Saint Cuthbert's record hop was a different kettle of fish.

Father Mark was in regular attendance at the hops, because he had been made aware, from some source or other, that smooching and snogging was creeping in because the other venues were allowing it. You see, the problem had arisen because the smooch was the newest slow dance which had come from America and which necessitated the boy to hold the girl with both hands round her waist and the girl to hold the boy with both hands round his neck.

This meant the couple had to adopt the position of full frontal contact. I had no problem with that; in fact it was the perfect position for a good snog, and that was considered not really proper behaviour on the dance floor. In fact, it was positively banned at Saint Cuthbert's hops. You were allowed to smooch as long as you didn't actually make contact in the middle section. You had to leave, as I said before, an arm's thickness between your respective genitalia.

Father Mark had found a mission in his prudish life, namely to force dancers to keep their distance. He would take up his position on the periphery of the dance floor during the fast dances, the Jive and the Twist, but as soon as the tempo slowed down, the full hall lights were switched on and he did his 'roving interruptus' act, equipped with a broom handle. He followed couples round the dance floor and as soon as he spotted potential offenders, he homed in on them with his stick and forced them apart if necessary by placing the stick between them, and giving them one of his withering looks.

If he actually caught you snogging he'd physically throw you out of the hall, denouncing you as sinners and fornicators. This happened on many occasions, and due to his interference, numbers plummeted and the weekly record hop was permanently cancelled, which was a shame, because some kids were only allowed to go to the Saint Cuthbert's record hops because they were considered properly supervised. Now there would be nowhere for these kids to enjoy a good dance, unless they followed the rest of us who had discovered the newly-formed Friday night disco at Wyndham School in Egremont.

This was to be the most popular school disco of all time, and the only place to be on a Friday night. It was hot! The lighting was perfect; the school was brand new and the atmosphere in the hall was very avant-garde and rebellious. Not a single sign of a snooping adult, never mind a manic priest. You could smooch, snog and feel as many arses as you liked. I thought I'd died and gone to hell! Well, that's where I was sure I was bound for. The permissive society was being born here before my very eyes.

CHAPTER 50
SOMEWHERE OVER THE RAINBOW

I came across it just by accident. I'd gone for one of my long walks in the rain. I love walking with the rain pelting on my face and the wind buffeting me from side to side. In fact I love to walk whatever the weather and its best on your own, nobody to distract you from the noises and smells of the countryside.

It must have been seven o'clock or so when I decided to slip out of bed and reach for my Wellington boots. Steven and Barry were still making sleeping noises, shifting about a bit and still locked into the fitful, could waken anytime sort of sleep. I had been wide wake for at least half an hour listening to the gentle summer rain brushing across our bedroom window, collecting in droplets on the concrete ridge and cascading them into the sill every now and then like somebody emptying a po from the room above only there isn't any room above.

I'm drifting back into my sleep. No, I'm not. I'm getting up. Bugger this for a game of dominoes. I've got things to do, places to go, people to meet. Well actually, today I don't want to meet anybody. I want to be alone. Who was it said that? Some old bird in a film I think. Well I know how she feels. Sometimes you just want to see nobody and speak to nobody,. Except Mam. I always want to see her. She's great. She's spot on.

She sometimes sees me in one of my far away moods and says, 'What's the matter, lad, you're miles away?. Are you OK?' And looks at me with such kindness and love in her eyes. And I'll say, 'Yeh, Mam. I'm fine. I'm just thinking.' And we pass a glance at each other and there's no need for any more words. Words can sometimes clutter things up. There's no need for too many of them. That's how Mam and me are.

This morning I wasn't even going to get the pleasure of a thoughtful glance from Mam. I got dressed, cleaned my teeth, didn't bother with a wash. I donned my wellies and slipped out of the back door like a thief in the night.

I had on my florescent orange nylon anorak and Dad's deerstalker hat. Once I get into the fells, I will be the only thing, excluding the Great Wall of China, visible from the moon. I love clothes that make a statement. This is hardly fashion victim stuff mind you. I'm in my 'must be noticed in the mist on the fells' fashion phase; a sensible attitude to fell walking; my latest obsession.

I know I should have left a map of my route and expected time to return on the kitchen table for would be rescuers before I left, but I wasn't that obsessed. I took Granda Close's walking stick with me, the one he left Dad. He'd made it himself from a piece of blackthorn. It had a great feel to it with its smooth knob end. Mam says it was his Shillelagh, what ever that means.

Dad's a dab hand at making walking sticks. You can find him ratching round for hours in dykes when we're out for a walk, looking for that perfect branch joint with either a good right angle or a deformed ball-like joint like Granda's stick. He just uses them once and throws them away, it seems a terrible waste of effort, but that's Dad.

Mam says he's torture to live with because he changes his mind like the weather. He'll probably approve of my taking his deerstalker and Granda's stick, but he's not struck on the daglo anorak. He thinks everything bright coloured should be on a woman's back, not a man's or a lad's. He says orange is for Nancy boys, so he tries to ignore me when he sees me in my fell gear. Mam says to take no notice, he's old fashioned.

Its funny, Dad's been doing a bit of decorating for a lady at Rose Bank, Hensingham, and Mam says she knew her when she had nowt, and Dad says she used to trail Cleator backs when she was a wee lass with the snotters blinding her. They seem very scathing of the poor woman.

Apparently she's got a dinette and a bay window. What the hell is a dinette? Dad says he hasn't got a clue but she's told him she's got one and he's got it to decorate. Mind you, Dad could have got the word wrong, he's inclined to do that at times. He's always talking about people going to the Casuality department at Whitehaven Hospital, and according to him the council are taking all the tin sheeting fences down and replacing them with timber and making a hartitechical feature of them. Who knows?

I am passing by Winnie Burns' shop on the corner of Priory Drive and Ennerdale Road, looking like a Belisha Beacon she's giving the bread man hell about a crusty cob she didn't get the day before. The poor man's nearly reduced to tears. She's like Genghis Khan – you cross her at your peril.

Mind you, they haven't even noticed me. I'm not too confident in this orange anorak. If it can't attract the bread man and Winnie Burns in a light summer drizzle, how's it going to cope in a blizzard on Nannycatch Fell with a force nine gale behind it? I'll just have to hope I never need to find out.

I've decided on my route and I rather fancy that crusty cob from Winnie Burns' which she didn't get delivered. Should I ask her for it and a quarter of boiled ham, oh God, I wish I had the guts to. After the 'trial by bread' on the pavement, Winnie assumed her position behind the counter and greeted me with the details of her run-in with the bread man.

'I mean, I have to get my bread order complete, Sean, because I don't want to let my customers down. They depend on me being efficient and you just get let down all the time. What do you want, lad, are you going hiking?' (She's noticed my anorak. Thank God I won't perish in the snow.)

'Yes,' I say. 'I'm off round the back of Dent.'

'Well, you look the part. You've got all the gear, Sean. At least you'll never get lost in that windcheater.' (Windcheater, what the hell is a windcheater? It's an anorak.) She's amused by it, I'm sure, but I don't care. Winnie is always nice to me and I decided to confide in her.

'Winnie,' I say. 'Do you think this ANORAK is a bit loud?'

After a short pause, she said, very seriously, 'Not at all, lad. It's bright, but you need to be seen on the fells. You're taking a very responsible attitude, Sean, and I admire you for that, and for having the courage to wear it, lad.'

Well, I didn't know what the hell to make of that. Winnie suggests I take a pork pie and two bananas with me, plus a Kendal mint cake and three ice pops, unfrozen, to drink, for ease of carrying, rather than a bottle of lemonade. I accept her advice on the pie and fruit and decline the soft ice pops in favour of fresh water from a stream. I settle up with 1s 8d for the purchases, and just as I'm leaving the shop I turn round and ask Winnie if any of our lot are in during the day to let Mam know where I am going and I should be back by tea time.

She agrees to this and says she'll tell Auntie Lily because she'll be sure to be in for the crack on her way home from the Moor. Good, now I feel at ease with my day's walking. 'How's Papa, by the way?' she asks, as I shut the door behind me. 'Better, I think,' I gesture. The smell from Walkers bakery makes me want to start on my goodies before I even start off, but I resist. I know I will be hungry after two or three hours walking.

When you ascend the hill towards Wath Brow from Priory Drive along Ennerdale Road with Montreal and Ehenside school on your right, in the centre of your view is Wath Brow Mission, the subject of 'Matchstick Man', L S Lowry's painting. Cleator Moor is famous for producing the subject of three paintings by the eminent artist, and Miss Dempsey says Cleator Moor should make more of this great honour.

The Mission looks like a wedding cake decoration, it's almost too perfect. Situated exactly in the centre of the crossroads at the end of Ennerdale road, with Kinniside Kop and Dent making the perfect backdrop. Oh, I'm going all arty.

Well, you've got to pass Maggie Howland's and the Greyhound pubs to get to the mission. At this time in the morning the smell of stale beer and fags drifting from their open doors. As the cleaners splash Jay's fluid and empty the ash trays from the night before, a high state of artistic appreciation takes some conjuring up, but it can be done.

Why are there so many pubs on Cleator Moor? You've got to pass yet another pub called 'The Littlers Arms' before you finally escape Cleator Moor and slip with great ease down the steep hill to Low Wath and Hen Beck Bridge. The drizzle has stopped and a bright shaft of sun light forces itself through. This is where the real walking and smelling and hearing and looking starts.

Once over the bridge, continue left for a short while and turn right up past the White House, a huge buttress-fronted, white-painted house built by the water board to stand guard over and house the caretaker of the reservoir which it flanks. I just drift into automatic pilot at this point. It's the nearest thing to a perfect experience you could hope to have. Just to absorb the bombardment to the senses which I just allow to happen.

Words to describe this experience couldn't even scratch the surface, so I won't even try. Suffice to say I am eventually transported along flat fell around the back of Dent, floating through Lowther Park and taking the back of Dent from behind.

Skating past Samson's Rock over the soft moss and bracken and levitating all the way down stopping briefly to catch sight of the Scottish coast, the Isle of Man and something on the horizon that looks like a Chinese painting of a distant island.

It's just visible. A few dots, nothing more. It looks eerie, like a mirage. What the hell is it? I'm mesmerised. I've never seen it before. It's definitely land of some sort. Then suddenly it dawned on me. It's Ireland! It's Ireland!

The realisation leaves me feeling very emotional. I can't explain why. I don't understand why I feel such a deep sense of sadness at the sight of my ancestors' home land. It's almost as if something has stirred deep inside me and I can only slump to the ground and sink into the wet carpet of sparkling bright green moss and listen to the deep growling noises in my head. I feel as if somebody has got hold of my heart and is gripping it so tight I can't stand the pain. It's not a real pain. I'm not ill. I just feel wretched and very, very desolate. It's extraordinary.

It took a few minutes to pass and I realised I needed to eat my snack, and within seconds of eating my second banana I feel fantastic, no more sadness or feeling of despair. I couldn't understand any of it. Maybe I'd gone too long without food. I'd had no breakfast, not even a drink, and I must have been walking for a few hours. Maybe my blood sugar was low. Dad gets that sometimes. He says he 'goes all wallow'. Maybe I've gone 'all wallow', or my ancestors were crying out to me when I saw Ireland, telling me I should be in Ireland where I belong, not walking through the English countryside, like one of them. I keep feeling very high then very low. I got back onto my feet and slowly moved down the fellside towards Black Howe farm and Cleator village.

At the bottom of the fell, just as you reach the fell road above Black Howe Farm, you have to climb a stile to access the road. I stood on top of the stile and looked back up Dent where I'd just walked.

Immediately in front of me was an old hencoop on wheels with a fine wire netting hen run in front of it and it had four banty cock chickens and four white banty hen chickens. The cocks were beautiful; multicoloured browns, greens and reds. The hens were pure white and they seemed to be dancing with each other, moving around in the confined space in perfect formation. The wood behind them was all lit up with brilliant sunlight and the fell side had lovely sharp patches of colour like a gaudy Patchwork quilt. It almost looked like technicolor. What the hell was it all saying to me?

I got back on to the fell road and walked the rest of the mile and a half or so back to our house without noticing anything at all. When I got back to Seaview Place, Barry met me at the back door and said, 'Sean, Mam and Auntie Lily have gone to Nana Heron's, Papa's dead!'.

I couldn't take it in at first. How could our wonderful Grandfather be dead? He was going to live forever, or that's what we all thought. I felt once again that sense of desolation I had experienced on the fells. Had I had a premonition of Papa's death or had I just had a realisation at the exact time of his death? I had received a message from him I felt sure, but I was confused as to exactly what the message was.

I was to understand that message, much later in my adult life.

CHAPTER 51
PAPA'S DEAD

The date was 13th of August 1963. He was seventy-nine years old and would have had a good ten years left in him if it hadn't been for that new car, Mam said. Papa had bought one of the first Minis ever made in 1959. It was bright red and unlike any other car that came before it. It was a symbol of the changing times. Minimalist; chic in miniature. It was small, compact and very fast.

Papa loved it but it only had two doors. He kept it for just over a year and sold it simply because Nana had to disembark every time Papa stopped to give someone a lift, which was practically every journey he made. He'd always had large four-door cars, but this new mini had really taken his fancy. It had, however been a mistake. The new car Papa had bought just a few months before his death had been a Hillman Minx. Four doors, of course. A lot bigger than the mini, but not as big as many of his previous Austins and Fords.

Cars were his passion, and this one made a large contribution to his death. He'd always garaged his cars and his garage was quite a walk from his house. This meant that he'd often got a soaking going for or putting away the car, and besides he was getting to an age where he didn't always feel like a walk to the garage site every time he used the car, especially late at night.

He decided to erect a garage in the front of the garden. Well, the access would be from the front of the house, the garage would be situated at the side of the house. He was still a fit man, or so we thought. He had several tons of hardcore delivered and he had handballed most of it himself using a heavy concrete roller to compact it into the driveway.

He'd complained about pains in his left arm and was blaming the heavy steering on the new Hillman, compared with the Mini. This should have served as a warning to him to slow down, but he wasn't the kind of man to slow down. He'd only driven the car a handful of times when the first heart attack came. In fact, it wasn't until his first severe attack that the doctor told him he'd had several small heart attacks which he hadn't been aware of.

Papa was devastated. This man had not known illness in his entire seventy nine years. He'd always worked for himself and worked hard and long hours for too many years. He'd turned seventy before he retired from business and his last bout of manual labour had been his undoing. He laid in bed for three weeks then succumbed to a massive heart attack and died instantly. He had put all of his affairs in order and died surrounded by his family.

The family were inconsolable, I had never seen my Mam and Aunties display such grief and hysteria. They were totally devastated. Nana was the one that got the family through the terrible shock. She was the rock, the strong one. She comforted her daughters and son and their children, who all adored him. She insisted the women all had new black outfits for the funeral and organised the funeral breakfast in the top room of the Albert Hotel opposite our church at Brookside.

She presided over all the funeral arrangements and maintained her dignity and composure throughout. She was the Matriarch and how splendid she was. Everyone else was falling apart, but even though she loved him more than anybody and was going to be affected most by his death, was strong and very together. She was doing this for Papa and her children. The pain of seeing the distress this was causing my Mam and Aunties was almost too much to bear.

The man they loved and admired above all men had left them so abruptly.

A POEM BY W.H. AUDEN

Stop all the clocks, cut off the telephone, prevent the dog from barking with a juicy bone, Silence the pianos and with muffled drum, bring out the coffin, let the mourners come.

Let aeroplanes circle, moaning overhead, scribbling on the sky the message He is dead,

Put crepe bows round the necks of public doves, let the traffic policeman wear black cotton gloves.

He was my north, my south, my east, my west, my working week and my Sunday rest,

My noon, my midnight, my talk, my song. I thought that love would last forever, I was wrong.

The stars are not wanted now, put out every one. Pack up the moon and dismantle the sun,

Pour away the ocean and sweep up the wood, for nothing now can ever come to any good.

It was going to take a long time for Nana to mourn and come to terms with losing Papa.

CHAPTER 52
DEAD MEN'S SHOES

Auntie Winnie was particularly devastated by Papa's death because she'd come to rely on him in recent months. Since the death of her husband, Eddie Devoy six months before, Papa had taken on many of his duties. He'd died of cancer in the spring of that year. She had lost a husband who was only forty-five years old and her Dad within six months of each other. She was a widow at forty-two and looked ten years older than my Mam, who was five years older than her.

They had the Miller's Inn at Cleator, locally known as the 'Cellar'. They'd only been tenants for about three years before Eddie became ill. Actually, looking back, he'd probably been ill for longer but hadn't complained. Nobody realised.

Little things should have been a sign of his illness. He'd displayed an unhealthy pallor for a long time and he'd gone so very thin. Hindsight is a wonderful thing. People punish themselves for things they can only see in retrospect. It doesn't do any good; it only shifts the blame.

He'd worked at Sellafield as a welder. He'd worked for many years on the construction site, but he'd latterly been employed by BNFL and worked in 'wet suits' in highly contaminated areas. The suits were supposed to protect them from radiation when they were working in contaminated areas.

Eddie had been moved from 'the area' and been told to stay out for twelve months because he'd had a 'high dose' in one session. Foolishly, he was allowed back into 'the area' after just a few weeks and soon after succumbed to a throat infection which turned out to be cancer. He had to give up work at the Nuclear Plant but kept on the pub, which he loved.

Auntie Winnie hated the pub from the first time she set foot in it, but it had always been Eddie's dream, so she supported him in it. During the afternoons, Uncle Eddie had a lie down and Auntie Winnie and Uncle Faley shared the midday trade, which fortunately was usually light. Uncle Faley was actually my great uncle (Nana Heron's bachelor brother) who had lived with Auntie Winnie and Uncle Eddie for many years as a lodger.

He'd been retired from the pit for a number of years and was reliable for pulling the odd pint of beer but for little else. Auntie Winnie was glad of him at this time in her life and spoke of him with affection, always referring to him as 'poor Faley'. Anyhow, Faley had been asked by some inquiring customer if he was 'chucker-outer' and he'd famously replied 'we could do with a chucker-inner, never mind a chucker-outer'.

Auntie Winnie has given notice to the brewery and was, to say the least, disinterested in the life of a publican. She was just going through the motions until she could be legally released from the tenancy which would be shortly after Papa died.

It's strange how times of sadness can bring people together. Auntie Winnie (Mam's sister) and Auntie Maggie (Dad's sister) had not spoken for years due to a fall out over the kids. Mam was in an awkward position because she was very fond of Auntie Maggie and clearly loved her sister Auntie Winnie. She didn't subscribe to the 'kick one and they all limp' school of thought, which many of the Cleator Moor families adopted. She dealt with her dilemma by using diplomacy and not mentioning one to the other.

When we were checking on Auntie Winnie the night before Uncle Eddie's funeral, we were all surprised and delighted to find Auntie Maggie and Auntie Winnie clinging onto each other on Auntie Winnie's front step, breaking their hearts. Auntie Maggie had gone to see Auntie Winnie to make her peace and to tell her how sorry she was for her trouble. She left her a bunch of shamrock in a little posy and told Winnie she was praying to Saint Patrick for her.

Moving Statues

Auntie Winnie's daughter, Maureen, had just married an Ulster man, Norman Boyd, and his orange colours came out, to the surprise of the family. Auntie Winnie had a collection of holy statues scattered round the old pub house. The usual Saint Martin (The Black Saint), Our Lady of Lourdes and a particularly large statue of the sacred heart, among others.

Of late, she often found the statues either turned facing the wall or laid on their sides. She was perplexed by this and asked everyone in the house if they knew any reason for it and was beginning to read some weird significance into the moving statues. Mam and Dad were helping out behind the bar at night and Dad had to go into the house to get some change when he discovered the reason for the moving statues.

He'd gone into the living room and saw Norman (Maureen's husband) laying our Lady's statue on its side and confronted him. Norman said, 'Jay, I just hate these statues. I'm an Irish Protestant, an Orangeman, and you have no idea how much I loathe all this lot!' So Dad had said, 'Norman, there's an old saying, "When in Rome, do as the Romans do." Winnie has given you a good home here, and you should treat her things with respect. Now let that be the finish, do you hear me, Norman, or you and me will have a fall out. That lass has been through enough lately without you piling it on.' Norman agreed to leave the statues alone and Dad promised to say no more about it, so it remained a mystery for a long time to come.

Auntie Winnie had finally started sorting out Uncle Eddie's clothes and gave Dad a pair of black, suede shoes. People liked to recycle things because things were hard come by and couldn't just be thrown away. Dad didn't want the shoes, you could tell. He accepted them and even remarked on how much wear was left in them, but he would never wear them. I saw him kneeling in front of the wardrobe in Mam and Dad's bedroom one Saturday night when he was going out for a pint. He had the black, suede shoes in his hands and he was crying. When he came back down stairs, his eyes were all red and he had on a pair of his own brown, leather shoes.

When he was questioned by Mam about why he had never worn the shoes, he just said they nipped his bunions and she could give them to a rummage sale.

CHAPTER 53
A TOUCH OF ANGINA

Nana Heron's got a touch of angina. She's been told by Doctor Strain to take it easy and not to walk too far. She's receiving guests in bed. She gets a lot of visitors. I've gone up to see her and to take her a magazine rack I'd made in woodwork. Mam said it would cheer her up. It was made with pieces of half inch dowels to form the rack front and it could be wall-mounted or stood on the floor.

It had taken me a full term to make the magazine rack. In fact, I'd gone back after school for the last month to finish it and I was very proud of my handiwork. Nana was delighted; you'd have thought I'd given her a thousand pounds. Aunty May had told me I could take it up to show her, but not to stay long for fear of tiring her out. Mam says that that's what's wrong with her, she's just tired out. She's spent her whole life working hard after leaving school at thirteen to look after her family. Her mother had died of cancer, she was only thirty-three, and Nana was the oldest of six.

She was in pensive mood, I could tell. She looked very regal sitting up in her bed, in her pink housecoat. One of the neighbours had been in and done her hair. She said she regretted having had it cut (she'd had her hair up in a bun until lately) because it was harder to look after, short. She had a perm put in it, and although she was in her night clothes, she looked years younger than she used to with the severe bun and a hairnet.

She was looking round the room and at her new magazine rack. I said, 'Where will you put the rack, Nana?'

And she said, 'I'll put it next to the chimney breast in the recess beside my chair, Son, so I can reach it without having to get up. It'll be just grand for me there.' And thanked me again for thinking about her.

I said, 'Nana, do you not get bored being in bed all day?'

And she gave out a wee laugh. 'Not at all, son. I've got plenty to occupy me mind, and this is a nice room to be laid up in.'

It was a nice room. It had a modern bedroom suite and the bed had a low headboard and a beautiful pink satin eiderdown. Nana looked as if she was sitting up in a great giant blancmange. I said, 'Was this

Papa's bedroom, Nana?'

And she said, with a rather puzzled look on her face, 'No, lad. Stephen slept in the next room.' They both got a better night's sleep that way.

She called Papa Stephen. I'd never heard her call him Stephen before, in fact I'd never heard her mention him since his death, and I wanted to talk about him to her. I said, 'Do you miss him, Nana?' She smiled at me. Her whole face lit up and she answered me, 'By God, I do that, lad. He was the best man to ever walk across Cleator Moor market square. We had fifty five years together; fifty five happy years, Sean, and now he's gone. But I've got all the memories and that keeps me going. I think about him a lot, but we all have to die, son, and I'll be with him in heaven some day, please God.'

She firmly believes that they will be together again in heaven. I wonder how she can be so sure. There's absolutely no doubt in her mind, you can tell. I'm not so convinced about the hereafter. I'm going through a doubting phase. I've not discussed it with anybody; I just hope it goes away. Life's simpler when you can just accept what you've always believed in, but sometimes you question it in your mind. I mean, what if there is no heaven – or hell, for that matter? Nobody knows for certain (except Nana), and after all, nobody comes back from the dead to tell us. We just accept it, or most of the time that is, and life settles much more easily on my shoulders when I'm not in a doubting phase.

She looks so fragile sitting up in her housecoat. Bedclothes make you seem vulnerable during the day; they make you look as if you only have a half life; as if you could be snuffed out at any minute. I hope she soon gets better and back downstairs.

She looked at me as if she'd just come back from a long journey. We'd been quiet for a few minutes, both lost in our separate thoughts, and she said, 'You know, Sean, it's nice to have time to yourself. Our May looks after me – she's a good lass. I want for nothing here. I have the newspapers and me rosary beads and plenty of visitors. The days go in. But I do miss being busy. When we had the business and May had the confectioner's shop on Jacktrees Road, we hardly had time for a good scratch, and I really enjoyed that life. But now I have all the time in the world to reflect on the happy times and get a bit of pampering, so who am I complain? You know what I miss the most, being upstairs?'

And I said, 'No, what, Nana?'

And she smiled, 'You won't believe this, but the thing I miss most is making me pasties on Tuesday mornings. I like nothing better than having the kitchen to meself and peeling the onions and rolling the pastry and feeling the fresh soft mince between me fingers, and the smell of the pastry when I open the oven door - it's the simple things you miss the most. But I'm not intending to lie here for ever, you know. Doctor Strain says just another week and I can get back to me kitchen again. May does all the housework and all the washing up, so I'll soon be back to me wee bit of shopping and cooking, please God'.

She's great, isn't she? She's just a whole life packaged up in a pink room, not quite ready to be posted. The string's on, but the sealing wax hasn't been melted yet. There's so much I want to ask her about her life, and about Papa – what was he really like?

May poked her head round the bedroom door, carrying a tray with Nana's tea on it – ham sandwiches and a buttered scone, a pot of tea and some chocolate biscuits for me.

She looked at Nana and said, 'How are you, Mammy?'

And Nana looked back at her and said, 'I'm nicely, May, Sean and me are having a lovely wee crack.'

May seemed at ease (which for her was saying something), and she set the tray down on the bedside table. She produced a small tray with short stubby legs that folded out onto Nana's lap and said, 'Sean, if you're staying for a wee while longer I'll just slip up to the Moor for Mammy's prescription. John's here and he'll run me up. I'll get a few things at the Co-op, Mammy, while I'm out.'

So I was being left in charge to take care of Nana for a few precious minutes and I was relishing every second of it. Nana settled down to eat her tea. She ate bird-like, just pecking at the bread, not really relishing it, it was just fodder. She had no appetite, she was just going through the motions. She finished her scone and wiped her mouth with her napkin and asked me to put the tray on the floor out of her way. This done, she folded her arms and said, 'Now, what can I tell you about Papa?'

I thought for a moment, because I couldn't think of anything specific I needed to know, I just wanted to be reminded of him; I wasn't ready to let him go yet, so I said, 'Tell me about him when he was young.'

She settled back on her pillows and her face was animated. She started by telling me how hard-working he had always been, building up his business from nothing, until he ended up with a small fleet of buses and taxis. Her Dad had died just before they got married, and the chip shop was sold and Nana had a bit of money, so Papa set himself up in the motor business and it grew over the years. When some Cleator Moor people were half starved to death during the Depression, they thrived and brought up a well-fed, healthy family, except for Maggie, who died at twenty-three from TB. Nana said he'd broken his heart over poor Maggie, Lord rest her.

The war came and brought plenty of work for Papa taking the miners back and forth to the pits, and life was good. She remembered having a special meal for Papa's fiftieth birthday and Aunty May hadn't anywhere near enough meat coupons to buy a decent piece of brisket, so she'd bought a piece of pork on the black market. They were all sitting round the table in the front parlour, Papa admiring the handsome cut of pork. He asked May how she'd managed to save up the meat coupons for the pork, and she said, 'Oh, Daddy, there's ways and means,' knowing his dislike of black market goods.

He placed the carving knife and fork down on the table, looked at Nana and said, 'You haven't used coupons for this meat, May Lizzie, have you?'

And she'd said, 'No, Stephen, May bought it from a farmer, specially for your birthday.' Papa said, 'That was very thoughtful of you, May, but I'll not be eating any black market meat. Our lads are fighting for our future and they won't be eating roast pork today.'

'He took some vegetables and pickled beetroot and ate his meal alone. He was as straight as a die, Sean. He wouldn't borrow money for a new taxi or bus, he'd save until he could pay for it outright. The bank manager was always telling him he should use their money to expand, but he wouldn't. He hated debt. He wasn't much of a businessman; he left all the book work to me and May, and wouldn't take any advice on financial matters, but he was happy at his work, and that's what matters at the end of the day, and we did alright.

He looked after his family and he loved his grandchildren, that's where he got his pleasure. He liked nothing better than to take a car full of the grandchildren to Nethertown or round to the docks.' (These were events that I took part in on numerous occasions). 'You were his life, and he'd give you his last penny. Now, I think I've talked enough now, lad, so why don't you read me a wee bit out of the Whitehaven News before May gets back. I struggle with the size of the pages when I'm in bed. I like to spread it out on the kitchen table, so I don't get it read while I'm in bed'.

I read the births, deaths and marriages, which Nana listened to with great interest, tutting at the deaths she hadn't heard about, then I read some readers' letters and when I looked up she was fast asleep. I folded the paper up, took the tray away and lingered at the bedroom door for a few seconds, watching her sleeping soundly and thinking how much I loved her.

CHAPTER 54
THERE'S A PRICE TO PAY FOR
STANDING YOUR GROUND

I had wasted much of my time at school. I take full responsibility for this. The Secondary School system which was in operation at the time gave a very broad-based education. Secondary pupils weren't expected to be academics; the true academics were the successful students who had gained a pass for the grammar school at eleven years old. I wasn't among them.

When I first went to Secondary School in 1959 I was placed in the A stream along with my twin brother Stephen and every year, when the end of year exams came round both Stephen and I engaged in a week or so of panic revision for the exams and always managed a respectable exam result. This rush of interest in our studies, for my part, was mainly due to my misplaced pride, because I couldn't face the ignominy of going down to the B form. I had much more ability than I had a mind to display. There seemed to be too many distractions from boring lessons and no real incentives or goals to work toward.

I, like all the rest of my Secondary contemporaries, expected to leave school at fifteen and gain useful employment in the booming jobs market of the time. Nobody, to my certain knowledge, left school without gaining employment of some sort or other. We weren't being tailored to take GCEs, because Saint Cuthbert's didn't have a fifth form until my last year, when it was first introduced as an option, so what was there to aim for?

Toward the middle of my last year, around about January 1963, I suddenly realised I could stay on for the fifth year and go on to take some GCEs. Encouraged by Mr Monaghan, our English teacher, and others who were trying to establish a fifth form, and I decided I'd give it my best shot and stay on at school for an extra year. My parents were neither for it or against it. It was my decision.

The new fifth form was being put in place, and the mechanics of it were a bit haphazard to say the least, because some of the old guard were against it, namely Miss Cunningham, Drac. The new fifth form candidates, which included myself and Stephen plus a handful of our classmates, were given a pep talk by Mr Monaghan and told we would be expected to give our all to this new school enterprise. In return for their part, the staff that is, would treat us more as adults, befitting our status as fifth-formers.

We would decide, with advice from staff, the subjects we would be likely to be successful in and limit these main subjects to a maximum of three. My subjects were English Language, English Literature and Woodwork. Woodwork was one of the subjects I had shown particularly good promise in, and I enjoyed very much, having made many items over my four years at school, including a bookcase, magazine rack, lamp stand, raffia-topped oak stool and many more smaller items.

We were given work to study on our main subjects and, when we weren't actually in a specific lesson, we could do our independent studies in the library. Because this new venture had been introduced mid-term, we were told to abandon our original timetable and were based mainly in the school library, as no proper fifth form room was available at the time.

During one of our first free periods a handful of us were getting on quietly with our studies when suddenly, and very noisily, Drac thundered through the double doors of the library. It was my bad luck to be seated nearest to the library doors when she burst through. We all looked round in surprise and she homed in on me. She was in an obvious state of rage. Her voice was quaking when she asked me what I thought I was doing in the library when I should have been in her geography lesson.

I was much taken aback, because I had decided to drop geography as a GCE subject and I was under the impression, after discussion with Mr Monaghan, that I was to concentrate only on my chosen subjects until further notice. I explained to Drac that I was not taking geography for GCE and so wouldn't be attending her lessons any more and was about to explain that I had clearance from Mr Monaghan to be here during my free periods but was not given the chance.

She suddenly erupted into a full onslaught directed at me in particular because I was nearest to her. She said, 'Nobody drops my subject without full consultation with me, boy. Now, get out of here and go to your geography lesson now.' Her eyes were wild and her nostrils were flared with rage.

I remained seated and quite calmly told her I was in the place I was supposed to be, and she should go and see Mr Monaghan if she didn't believe me. We had obviously been caught in the cross-fire of some big political battle between Miss Cunningham and Mr Monaghan, and I was about to be the first victim. She rushed towards me and I flinched to avoid what looked to me to be a punch she was aiming at me.

I stayed put and she composed herself and said, still in a quaking voice, 'I'll tell you for the last time, get out of here and go to the geography room now – all of you.' I was aware of some movement from behind me, but the words Mr Monaghan had said were emblazoned on my mind: we would be treated as adults, befitting our status as fifth-formers. I wasn't prepared to be intimidated by this pompous, bullying dinosaur. I remained silent and seated. I was prepared to face the consequences of my refusal to obey her in what I expected to be a democratic system at a later enquiry. I wasn't prepared for a physical attack.

She pounced on me and literally dragged me off the chair by my hair. She continued to drag me out of the library while I struggled to free myself from her grip. By this time she was screaming at me to follow her. We were now in the corridor and Mr Heaslip, the new headmaster, was standing by his office door opposite the library and shouting at Miss Cunningham to let the boy go.

She released her grip on my hair and stood beside me with a handful of my hair in her fist. She rushed past Mr Heaslip towards the staff room and he shouted to me to wait in his office while he ran after Miss Cunningham. I sat down on the chair in front of his desk and was in a state of shock. I was trembling and hardly able to contemplate what had happened.

In due course, after about ten minutes, Mr Heaslip came into the office and said to me in a very calm and somewhat comforting voice, 'Sean, Miss Cunningham has been under a lot of strain. Her father was ill and she wasn't herself, I hope you can understand. And I can assure you this won't happen again. You can go home now, and if your parents would like to come and see me I'll explain the situation to them. Now, why don't you go home and come back tomorrow? You needn't be afraid of any reprisals, I can assure you of that. Are you alright? Would you like to go to the rest room and have a cup of tea, or maybe a lie down? What do you think?'

I was still stunned and can remember calmly saying to him, 'I'm OK, Mr Heaslip. I thought I was doing the right thing. I didn't mean to upset Miss Cunningham.'

He said, 'No, I'm sure you didn't. Things have got a bit out of hand here, but we'll get it sorted out, don't you worry.'

I didn't go home straight away. I took myself for a walk down to the beck and tried to make some sense of it all. I found myself feeling sorry for Miss Cunningham and thinking that if only I'd done what she told me I could have taken it up with Mr Monaghan later and avoided the whole thing. Why did I have to be the one to make a stand? I felt to a large extent that I'd been at fault and I should apologise to Miss Cunningham and I felt sympathy for her personal circumstances.

I eventually went home and told my mother what happened, and she asked me how I felt about it all. She was initially upset about my being violently attacked, but after my explanation about her father, and Mr Heaslip asking me to try to understand her situation, Mam decided not to go to school and make a fuss. The poor woman was obviously in a bad way about her father. We should be charitable and not make matters any worse for her. She gave me a letter she had written to Mr. Heaslip to give to him personally which explained how she was aware of Miss Cunningham's personal circumstances and no further action would be taken on her part.

Mr Heaslip in turn gave me a letter of apology from him to me and thanked my mother for her understanding. Miss Cunningham was missing from school for several days and on her return she seemed completely oblivious of the whole event and made no reference of it to me. It was as if nothing had happened. Mr. Monaghan, on the other hand, told me I should have done what I had been told to do by Miss Cunningham. She was a senior member of staff and I should have respected her authority. I should have gone to her lesson and afterwards gone to see him with my grievances. This would have avoided the nasty scene. I felt suitably chastised and a little bit better, if not slightly confused by his reaction.

This episode had helped me make my mind up to leave school. I had lost faith in the system and could feel the undercurrents of discord which existed between the staff and students, which was not conducive to serious studies on my part. I had already had interviews, all in good trades – motor mechanics, electrical engineering and joinery. I had been accepted by a garage in Whitehaven, but I didn't really fancy it. What I really wanted was joinery.

CHAPTER 55
THE CANADIAN DREAM

I was steadily showing an interest in, of all places, Canada. The reason being, one of Dad's cousins, Derek, had emigrated there. He and his wife, Hilda, had lived in Dagenham since Derek's father, my grandfather's brother had moved there before the war. They had all found work in the big Ford car factory and Mam and Dad had lived there when they first got married. Dad had a really good job in the ford works and both he and Mam had loved living there. Unfortunately, in the late forties accommodation was practically impossible to come by because of the devastation in the London suburbs, so they returned to Cleator Moor after a year and the birth of Barry, my brother.

Mam and Dad were in touch with Derek and Hilda, who were their age and had taken a keen interest in their move to Canada. I looked forward to reading their infrequent letters. They lived in Winnipeg, Manitoba, and the building industry where Derek worked was crying out for tradesmen and also trainees. Derek had suggested that maybe one of the twins might consider going out to train in the building trade.

They particularly wanted apprentice carpenters. He had indicated that he and Hilda would be prepared to sponsor one of us to come out. That would mean we would live with them and work with Derek making timber-framed houses. The Canadian government were running a scheme where they paid the tradesmen and trainees travel expenses and guaranteed them work to come to. If a Canadian family were prepared to stand as guarantors or sponsors, the applicants received preferential consideration.

Somehow, once the bandwagon started moving, there was no jumping off it. I was the natural choice between Stephen and me; firstly because I was practically inclined and secondly, Stephen refused to be in the running, stating he'd rather slit his throat than emigrate to Canada. So if one of us was to take up the very generous offer of Derek and Hilda, the choice as to who it would be was an easy one.

I felt myself being swept along on the wave of enthusiasm that was being generated. I could see myself in the new world of central

Canada. The feeling of being a part of a newly-developing country was appealing to me. I had that sense of adventure in me that my forbears must have had coming to England in the long-ago days of the Industrial Revolution. I decided I was going for it. Mam and Dad had put no pressure on me at all. They both approved of my decision and encouraged me in it; it would have been just the same if I had decided not to go. They were just happy to see us doing what we wanted for ourselves.

Somehow the next few months absolutely flew by. The letter telling Derek and Hilda that I had decided to come to Canada was sent early January, 1964, and by April my confirmation of acceptance had arrived and a ticket for my sea journey to Canada arrived a week later, dated 25th April. I was to sail from Portsmouth on the P&O liner, Lady Jest, to arrive three days later in Montreal via Greenland. Mam and Dad were to accompany me to Portsmouth.

My luggage was sent by rail three days before I was due to sail. I said all my goodbyes to my grandparents and relations and friends amid a sea of tears, but somehow I felt no sense of regret or emotion, except when I had to say goodbye to my brothers and sister. That was hard. I was going like a lamb to the slaughter. Dad had borrowed Uncle Robbie's car to drive me to Portsmouth. He'd not long had his nippy Morris 1000 and in fact it still smelled new inside.

I can't remember actually leaving our house at Seaview Place. It was all a bit of a blur. I blocked it out. I just remember seeing all the neighbours standing in their front gardens waving me off, and Mrs. Pooley was crying as we passed her on Priory Drive. Winnie Burns was standing on the step of her shop at the top of Priory Drive and she waved and blew me a kiss. Mam was crying for the first time, and Dad said, 'Aye, they'll miss you, lad, that's for sure,' his voice tapering off as he finished speaking.

I felt no sense of regret leaving the only place I'd known and been happy in all my life, just an overwhelming feeling of excitement at the prospect of what lay in front of me. The thought of four and a half days at sea with possible high spring tides and force nine gales (in spite of the fact that I got seasick on Lake Windermere) left me undaunted.

I wanted to stretch myself; to go to places I thought I could only dream about. Places like Niagara Falls, North America and Alaska, all within easy reach of Winnipeg. If I didn't like carpentry I could be a lumberjack, or a Canadian Mountie. Mind you, I'm only five foot six and eight stones in weight, but hell, I'm still only fifteen. I've got years of growth left. I could end up six feet tall and twenty stones. Who knows?

The journey to Portsmouth, passing through practically every town in England, took an agonising twelve hours. Remarkably, I hadn't been sick once, or even felt sick. We'd stopped loads of times on the journey and our last stop was in Oxford. It was about seven o'clock at night. Dad needed a pint and I saw for the first time the awe-inspiring spires of the cathedral and university colleges silhouetted in the dusky evening sky. I thought I was in a foreign land already.

The ship was due to sail on the midnight tide and I had to be on board by ten o'clock, so that left us with a little time to wander round Oxford and take in the history and heritage of the very English surroundings, including the university students riding round on their bikes with their caps and gowns flowing behind them as they dodged the pedestrians taking photographs, and gazing at the amazing buildings.

Dad knew his way around Oxford, because he'd been stationed nearby for a short time during the war when he was doing his training, and had rejoined the regiment after the war to be demobbed. So he was interested to see the rejuvenation from the bombing it had taken during the war. It looked like it had never seen any enemy bombs. Certainly, all the medieval colleges and chapels were well intact.

It was time to leave Oxford, and a sense of unease suddenly came over me. In the space of twelve hours I had been given a crash course in the British way of life. I'd seen small industrial towns, like Preston and Doncaster, and the beautiful green countryside between the towns and villages, not like the dramatic Lakeland landscape, but the soft rolling countryside of Lancashire and the flat miles and miles of carefully clipped hedges and square fields of the southern counties, and now the mind-blowing Gothic towers of Oxford.

I suddenly had a new perspective on this England which I was about to leave behind. I felt a sudden sense of panic come over me. I'd started the day feeling certain that this was what I wanted. I had been in no doubt as to whether or not I was doing the right thing, but within only a dozen or so hours I was beginning to have doubts.

For the first time in the four months since I had first started thinking about Canada I began to question if in fact it was what I really wanted.

Suddenly I thought about Nana Heron's words to Mam. She said, thinking I couldn't hear, 'Eileen, has Sean thought this out properly, lass? You know what a dreamer he is.'

And Mam had said, 'Mammy, he's talked about nothing else since Derek's letter. It's definitely what he wants.'

Mam was right. I had spoken of nothing else. I was completely carried away with the idea, but Nana was also right. I was a dreamer. I saw things through rose-coloured glasses, but I had the ability to make them work. At least in the past I had. But this was a mega dream, and I suddenly thought, 'What if I can't make it work?'

I took in none of Mam and Dad's conversation during the remaining journey from Oxford to Portsmouth, I just became aware of the signposts suddenly displaying the signs for Portsmouth. I felt no sense of panic, which I surely should have. Mam and Dad were completely oblivious of the fact that I was having grave doubts about what was happening to me.

I started to think about what I was giving up. I'd only previously focused on what I was going to gain by going to Canada; I hadn't tried to balance it against what I was giving up. I had a complete mental block regarding the positive aspects of my life in England. I had my family, of course; I had friends; I had my love for the fells and everything outdoors; I had a social life – dancing, socialising with school mates and my sometimes serious courting. What if the Canadians have no sense of fashion? Or no sense of humour? I hadn't met a Canadian.

Rapidly I was having serious doubts about Canada, and here I was within ten miles of the most irreversible decision of my life. I looked at Mam and Dad and thought how compliant they had been to my wishes; how supportive they had been and how strange to think that I was unsure, yet they were taking me swiftly on to a destiny I was increasingly unsure of.

That was the moment. Fifteen minutes from the quayside I said, in a very strong and unemotional voice, 'I've changed my mind. I'm not going to Canada.'

Mam shot her head round to the back of the car where I was seated and said, 'What did you say?'

I said, 'I'm sorry, Mam, but I'm not going to Canada.'

Dad didn't say a word, he just pulled off the road into a lay-by and I could see the ships and tankers in the distance. They looked as if they were hanging from the sky. I couldn't actually see the sea, just the huge ships. Dad very calmly said, 'I'll tell you what, lad. We'll have a drink of lemonade and a sandwich. You're probably hungry and you might not get a meal on the ship for a few hours. Then you'll feel alright. You're just a bit panicky.'

Mam looked at me while she poured some lemonade into a plastic cup and said, 'You'll be OK, lad. Try not to think of the size of the ship, that's probably what's put you off.'

I knew there was no persuading me, no matter what they or anybody else said to me. They both tried for a good hour, reassuring me I was only panicking, and as soon as I was on board the ship (which I should have been twenty minutes ago) I would be fine. I just glazed over. I said, over and over again, 'I've changed my mind.'

Dad, by this time, had driven the car to the emigrations office and customs and was physically pulling me out of the car. I stood on the dockside and refused to move a single step nearer the customs office. I kept climbing back into the car and Dad kept pulling me back out. He wasn't mad, he was just very calm and trying to cajole me. It was no good.

In the end Mam tried another tack. She said, 'What about Derek and Hilda? What are we going to say to them after all the trouble they've gone to, sponsoring you and making all the arrangements?'

I said, 'I'll write to them and say I'm sorry, but I'm not going.' I just knew it was not what I wanted.

Eventually Mam said, 'It's a bloody pity you hadn't realised you didn't want to go before we set off. Have you any idea how hard this had been for all of us? Get back into the car before I slap your face.'

I did as I was told and we all sat in silence for some time, Mam eventually crying and saying how she hadn't wanted me to go in the first place, but I had been determined. How could I have been so sure I wanted to go and then change my mind so quickly? I couldn't explain. I was too embarrassed to say I didn't want leave her and my Dad and Barry and Stephen and Margaret. We didn't have the words for that sort of conversation, I just said I realised I hadn't thought it through. It had all happened so quickly, and now I was here I was sure I didn't want to go to Canada.

That being said, Dad turned round and said, 'Sean, this is your very last chance. Are you going, or are we on our way back home?'

And I answered, 'Back home, Dad.'

Very little was said on the homeward journey. They had planned to stay overnight in a boarding house, but Dad said he wouldn't sleep so we might as well drive back home tonight, which we did, and I resumed my life in Cleator Moor without any bother. When anybody asked me about what happened to Canada I'd just say, things just didn't work out, and leave it at that.

CHAPTER 56
THE BEATLES/REBELS
WITHOUT A CAUSE

The excitement of the early sixties was a phenomenon. The big band sound was outdated. Elvis was still big, but people like Cliff Richard, Chubby Checker and Roy Orbison had hit the pop scene, paving the way for the biggest explosion in popular culture of modern times, the Beatles.

We were in the thick of Beatlemania within a month of their arrival on the pop scene. I don't think anyone realised the impact four young lads from Liverpool would have on the adolescent population of Britain. They were treated like the long-awaited prophets of the Old Testament. 1960s Britain was the perfect receptacle for the Beatles, just like 1930s Germany was for Hitler.

The Beatles, for my generation, epitomised the mood change and rebellion that so many of us felt in the early 1960s. They spat in the eye of authority and told the old guard to piss off, and many of us followed suit. The social and political repercussions of Beatlemania were to be felt for many years to come, because we identified with so many of the things they sang about.

For the first time in history children didn't do what authority told them to do just because the authoritarians said it was right. We were developing a mind and an opinion of our own, and we were beginning to be vocal about it for the first time. Evolution had taken a major step forward. Unfortunately, many of us had opinions on subjects we knew very little about, but, because of the mood of the times, had been given a confidence to be vocal about our somewhat ill-informed opinions.

The Rebel Without A Cause

The rebel without a cause was born. People jumped on bandwagons because it was the thing to do. 'Ban the Bomb' marches, student demonstrations, Anti-Vietnam protests and the like were a good reason for young people to mass together and look cool, or so they thought.

Although I never found myself caught up in any of this, I saw my contemporaries and heard them sound off about the inequality of the masses and the downfall of the proletariat, and the boring, clichéd speeches of the political anarchists. We didn't have the benefit of hindsight, of course, but it's all very embarrassing looking back now. How could we have been so naïve? That was the Beatles for you.

We should have just enjoyed their music and knuckled down to a bit of hard work. Come to think of it, that is just what I did do. Well, almost.